£2.50

Doc Bog
Bale, Norfolk
August 2014

GW00456859

CARIBBEAN WRITERS SERIES

15

Selected Poetry

CARIBBEAN WRITERS SERIES

Selected Poetry

Derek Walcott

Selected, annotated and introduced by
Wayne Brown

HEINEMANN
LONDON . KINGSTON . PORT OF SPAIN

Heinemann Educational Books Ltd
22 Bedford Square, London WC1B 3HH
PO Box 1028, Kingston, Jamaica
27 Belmont Circular Road, Port of Spain, Trinidad

IBADAN NAIROBI
EDINBURGH MELBOURNE AUCKLAND
HONG KONG SINGAPORE KUALA LUMPUR NEW DELHI

ISBN 0 435 98747 X

Set, printed and bound in Great Britain by
Richard Clay (The Chaucer Press) Ltd,
Bungay, Suffolk

Contents

Introduction: A Note to Teachers

One often hears the complaint that Derek Walcott's poetry is 'difficult'. Though the note of resentment is seldom justified (it usually masks laziness or a kind of defiant philistinism on the plaintiff's part), still, it adheres to the truth: many of Walcott's poems *are* difficult. Their difficulty, however, is almost never due to any impulse towards obscurantism in a poet who, from the very beginning, has sought to write 'verse ... clear as sunlight', and only infrequently to some incoherence of thought or expression. Rather, it is the ineluctable product of a mind predisposed to obliquity and thrown back on its own resources by the absence of a West Indian literary tradition or any consensus of culture – an educated and embattled mind, engaged in true thinking (which is always difficult), aware of the revelatory power of metaphor, the solace of allusion, the economy and philosophical mischief of a pun – and prepared, in the face of a climate of often stultifying parochialism, to riffle the vast vocabulary and supple syntax of Unabridged English for help in tracking down and expressing some nuance of thought or feeling. A characteristic Walcott poem thus exhibits a sophistication of language and a density of meaning which can make the exploration of it as delightful an exercise for the adventurous reader as it must be repellent to the mentally staid.

There are writers – the Trinidadian novelist V. S. Naipaul is one – whose books, like a surveyor's measurements, constitute successive examinations, from different angles, of the same terrain. Derek Walcott's poems comprise the opposite: a study of different vistas from the same viewpoint – or rather (since over the years the poet's angle of vision has altered, in exact relationship to the evolution of his style) from the slowly evolving perspective of someone taking a stroll. The reader of the 200-plus poems (apart from juvenilia) which Walcott has so far published thus comes away from them with a sense of their author as an identifiable, consistent and maturing character using poetry to explore the manifold aspects of life in and around him.

Nonetheless, in Walcott's verse certain subjects recur oftener than others. Chief among these are West Indian history, politics and the West Indian landscape; the nature of memory, and of the creative imagination, and the relationship between them; the poet's own marriages and loves; his precocious and enduring awareness of Time, and of his eventual death. If in the poems these concerns often seem to yield their particulars and blur towards allegory (so that one is tempted to describe Walcott's main themes simply as the unwavering themes of all literature: love, war, exile and death) this is because Walcott writes as someone simultaneously aware of himself as individual and as archetype – as a man belonging to a certain race, region and age, and as a witness for mankind.

Ultimately, a poet's claim to stature depends upon his mastery of, and influence upon, the language in which he writes. Much has been written (see also the note to 'The Schooner *Flight*: Chapter 11') about Walcott's search for his 'true' voice – i.e. for a language forged from the different tongues which together make up the babble of West Indian history – and it is worth reflecting upon the ebullience and creative possibilities of a linguistically heterogeneous region like the Caribbean. Yet Robert Graves's early comment, that Walcott 'handles English with a closer understanding of its inner magic than most (if not any) of his English-born contemporaries', remains, after twenty years, probably the most pertinent single remark about his work. In that time Walcott has moved from a consuming predilection for the iambic pentameter (the main line of English verse, and a line in which this West Indian poet has always seemed wholly at ease) to a mastery of other metres and, most recently, to an unusually supple *vers libre* exhibiting many of the virtues (if occasionally the odd vice) of prose, so that today, employing a variety of metres and forms, he writes, in the words of one commentator, like someone who knows exactly what he is doing. This process he initiated by means of a conscious, indeed wilful, rebellion against the iambic pentameter (see note to 'The Cast-away'); yet one has the impression that the pentameter remains the natural vehicle for his sensibility. A Walcott poem which accepts its lineaments is almost never derailed.

Though it is a flexible line which easily accommodates the extremes of contemplative observation ('Deciduous beauty prospered and is gone') and ejaculatory slang ('Man, all the men in that damned country mad!') the pentameter has tended in recent times to reflect the irony and epigrammatic mischief of its eighteenth-century adherents rather than the measured, meditative minds of its major architects since Shakespeare: Milton, Wordsworth, Tennyson, Yeats. The bulk of Walcott's verse composed to this metre stands in opposition to this trend. In his hands the line is deliberately slowed, heightened and left open, the paragraph displacing the couplet or end-stopped line as the unit of thought. Detailing all the ways in which Walcott achieves these effects lies beyond the scope of this note, but one of them should be mentioned here, since it is also a defining characteristic of his style, and that is his instinctive subversion of those parts of speech which Auden has called the bane of English pentametrical verse: the definite and indefinite articles. In a Walcott poem, often as not, the definite article is displaced by the demonstrative 'that', particularizing its object and slowing speech; and the sense of the indefinite is heightened (and dramatized) by its replacement by the throwaway 'some', which likewise slows the line. It is not difficult to understand why in a generalizing, impatient age the sensibility behind such mannerisms should be defined – or should define itself – as conservative; or to deduce in what ways such a relationship between the poet and his audience is likely to influence, in its turn, the former's language, perspective and themes.

In itself, however, a catalogue of a poet's themes and metres is not a reliable indication of his true concerns and sensibility – there may be individual poems which are more or less emotionally ingenuous or structurally uneasy or internally discordant. In choosing these poems, therefore, I have tried to resist the temptation to produce a 'representative' anthology, preferring simply to select from those poems which struck me as best equipped to repay rereading. Because the real biography of a writer is to be found in the evolution of his style, I have left the poems in roughly the order of their original publication, rather than attempting to categorize them by theme or metre – though of course there exists a sound scholarly justification of the latter method. With the exception of those pertaining to the extracts of *Another Life** the notes which follow the poems are extensive but by no means exhaustive. Though aware that an approach which emphasizes either form or content at the other's expense greatly impoverishes the experience of poetry, I have come down rather heavily on the side of 'comprehension' – an unavoidable bias, I think, in a book of this kind. Even so, many of the notes will need the intercession of the teacher (I have assumed, for example, a knowledge of prosody which many students will not have had imparted to them, but without which, it seems to me, it is impossible to treat a poem as much more than an exercise in

---

* The extracts of the 150 page autobiographical poem, *Another Life* (Cape, 1973) presented the annotator with certain problems. A long poem moves at a comparatively leisurely or ponderous pace; thus, in order to maintain the fiction of their (structural) autonomy, it was necessary that the extracts themselves be lengthy. Furthermore, in attempting to annotate them on the same scale as the rest of the poems the annotator would have been forced constantly to refer beyond them to the unreproduced, and major, portion of the poem. All this prefigured a veritable cascade of notes, occupying perhaps as many pages as the extracts themselves, and beyond the scope of this book. For various reasons, the alternative (i.e. halving the number of extracts) seemed undesirable. I have therefore limited myself to the barest synopsis of each extract, along with the odd explanatory note. The teacher who is disinclined to treat these extracts merely as Material for Further Reading or as exercises in research ('who was Michelangelo?') may prefer to compare the language of different passages – the taut trimeters of 'E', for example, with the transparent prose of 'F' – or to select a few extracts for closer attention over a number of sessions. The interested student should be referred to the text in its entirety, and then, for help, to Edward Baugh's engaging explication of it, entitled *Derek Walcott: Memory as Vision: Another Life* (Longman, 1978). No serious analysis of the poem's form(s) has to my knowledge yet been published.

comprehension, and a botched and trivial 'comprehension' at that).

Finally, it is worth recalling Frost's dictum that a poem should 'begin in delight and end in wisdom'. Inherent in an annotator's task is the danger that in concentrating upon a poem's wisdom he may give short shrift to its delights. This is a trap which I have not always avoided.

I believe that the teacher who consciously counters this tendency of the notes, even going at times to the other extreme, will find his or her efforts rewarded; and that the student who submits to being led like a tourist among a poem's delights (its metaphors, its wit, some elegant turn of phrase or appropriate rhythm or rhyme) will ineluctably stumble upon its wisdom.

Selections from

In a Green Night

The Harbour

The fishermen rowing homeward in the dusk,
Do not consider the stillness through which they move,
So I, since feelings drown should no more ask
For the safe twilight which your calm hands gave.
And the night, urger of old lies
Winked at by stars that sentry the humped hills,
Should hear no secret faring-forth; time knows
That bitter and sly sea, and love raises walls.
Yet others who now watch my progress outward
On a sea which is crueller than any word
Of love, may see in me the calm my passage makes,
Braving new water in an antique hoax;
And the secure from thinking may climb safe to liners
Hearing small rumours of paddlers drowned near stars.

To a Painter in England

(for Harold Simmons)

Where you rot under the strict, grey industry
Of cities of fog and winter fevers, I
Send this to remind you of personal islands
For which Gauguins sicken, and to explain
How I have grown to learn your passionate
Talent with its wild love of landscape.

It is April and already no doubt for you,
As the journals report, the prologues of spring
Appear behind the rails of city parks,
Or the late springtime must be publishing
Pink apologies along the wet, black branch
To men in overcoats, who will conceal
The lines of songs leaping behind their pipes.

And you may find it difficult to imagine
This April as a season where the tide burns
Black, leaves crack into ashes from the drought,
A dull red burning, like heart's desolation.
The roads are white with dust and the leaves
Of the trees have a nervous, spinsterish quiet.
And walking under the trees today I saw
The canoes that are marked with comic names;
Daylight, St Mary Magdalen, Gay Girl.

They made me think of your chief scenes for painting,
Of days of instruction at the soft villa,
When we watched your serious experience, learning.
So you will understand how I feel lost
To see our gift wasting before the season,
You who defined with an imperious palette
The several postures of this virginal island,
You understand how I am lost to have
Your brush's zeal and not to be explicit.

But the grace we avoid, that gives us vision,
Discloses around corners an architecture whose
Sabbath logic we can take or refuse;
And leaves to the single soul its own decision
After landscapes, palms, cathedrals or the hermit-thrush,
And wins my love now and gives it a silence
That would inform the blind world of its flesh.

Ruins of a Great House

Stones only, the *disjecta membra* of this Great House,
Whose moth-like girls are mixed with candledust,
Remain to file the lizard's dragonish claws;
The mouths of those gate cherubs streaked with stain.
Axle and coachwheel silted under the muck
Of cattle droppings.

                    Three crows flap for the trees,
And settle, creaking the eucalyptus boughs.
A smell of dead limes quickens in the nose
The leprosy of Empire.

                    'Farewell, green fields'
                    'Farewell, ye happy groves!'

Marble as Greece, like Faulkner's south in stone,
Deciduous beauty prospered and is gone;
But where the lawn breaks in a rash of trees
A spade below dead leaves will ring the bone
Of some dead animal or human thing
Fallen from evil days, from evil times.

It seems that the original crops were limes
Grown in the silt that clogs the river's skirt;
The imperious rakes are gone, their bright girls gone,
The river flows, obliterating hurt.

4

I climbed a wall with the grill ironwork
Of exiled craftsmen, protecting that great house
From guilt, perhaps, but not from the worm's rent,
Nor from the padded cavalry of the mouse.
And when a wind shook in the limes I heard
What Kipling heard; the death of a great empire, the abuse
Of ignorance by Bible and by sword.

A green lawn, broken by low walls of stone
Dipped to the rivulet, and pacing, I thought next
Of men like Hawkins, Walter Raleigh, Drake,
Ancestral murderers and poets, more perplexed
In memory now by every ulcerous crime.
The world's green age then was a rotting lime
Whose stench became the charnel galleon's text.
The rot remains with us, the men are gone.
But, as dead ash is lifted in a wind,
That fans the blackening ember of the mind,
My eyes burned from the ashen prose of Donne.

Ablaze with rage, I thought
Some slave is rotting in this manorial lake,
And still the coal of my compassion fought:
That Albion too, was once
A colony like ours, 'Part of the continent, piece of the main'
Nook-shotten, rook o'er blown, deranged
By foaming channels, and the vain expense
Of bitter faction.

                    All in compassion ends
So differently from what the heart arranged:
'as well as if a manor of thy friend's . . .'

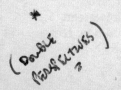
(Double
Meaninges?)

5

Tales of the Islands

CHAPTER III

la belle qui fut ...

Miss Rossignol lived in the lazaretto
For Roman Catholic crones; she had white skin,
And underneath it, fine, old-fashioned bones;
She flew like bats to vespers every twilight,
The living Magdalen of Donatello;
And tipsy as a bottle when she stalked
On stilted legs to fetch the morning milk,
In a black shawl harnessed by rusty brooches.
My mother warned us how that flesh knew silk
Coursing a green estate in gilded coaches.
While Miss Rossignol, in the cathedral loft
Sang to her one dead child, a tattered saint
Whose pride had paupered beauty to this witch
Who was so fine once, whose hands were so soft.

CHAPTER X

'adieu foulard ...'

I watched the island narrowing the fine
Writing of foam around the precipices then
The roads as small and casual as twine
Thrown on its mountains; I watched till the plane
Turned to the final north and turned above
The open channel with the grey sea between
The fishermen's islets until all that I love
Folded in cloud; I watched the shallow green
That broke in places where there would be reef,
The silver glinting on the fuselage, each mile

Dividing us and all fidelity strained
Till space would snap it. Then, after a while
I thought of nothing, nothing, I prayed, would change;
When we set down at Seawell it had rained.

A Careful Passion

Hosanna, I build me house, Lawd,
De rain come wash it 'way.
                    JAMAICAN SONG

The Cruise Inn, at the city's edge,
Extends a breezy prospect of the sea
From tables fixed like islands near a hedge
Of foam-white flowers, and to deaden thought,
Marimba medleys from a local band,
To whose gay pace my love now drummed a hand.
I watched an old Greek freighter quitting port.

You hardly smell the salt breeze in this country
Except you come down to the harbour's edge.
Not like the smaller islands to the south.
There the green wave spreads on the printless beach.
I think of wet hair and a grape red mouth.
The hand which wears her husband's ring, lies
On the table idly, a brown leaf on the sand.
The other brushes off two coupling flies.
'Sometimes I wonder if you've lost your speech.'
Above our heads, the rusty cries
Of gulls revolving in the wind.
Wave after wave of memory silts the mind.

The gulls seem happy in their element.
We are lapped gently in the sentiment
Of a small table by the harbour's edge.
Hearts learn to die well that have died before.
My sun-puffed carcass, its eyes full of sand,
Rolls, spun by breakers on a southern shore.
'This way is best, before we both get hurt.'
Look how I turn there, featureless, inert.
That weary phrase moves me to stroke her hand
While winds play with the corners of her skirt.

Better to lie, to swear some decent pledge,
To resurrect the buried heart again;
To twirl a glass and smile, as in pain,
At a small table by the water's edge.
'Yes, this is best, things might have grown much worse ...'

And that is all the truth, it could be worse;
All is exhilaration on the eve,
Especially, when the self-seeking heart
So desperate for some mirror to believe
Finds in strange eyes the old original curse.
So cha cha cha, begin the long goodbyes,
Leave the half-tasted sorrows of each pledge,
As the salt wind brings brightness to her eyes,
At a small table by the water's edge.

I walk with her into the brightening street;
Stores rattling shut, as brief dusk fills the city.
Only the gulls, hunting the water's edge
Wheel like our lives, seeking something worth pity.

Castiliane

I

The GOLONDRINA is a sour hotel,
Redeemed, like Creole architecture,
By its ornate, wrought-iron balcony;
A floral asterisk to grace a lecture
On 'Spanish Art In The Last Century'.
And though its rusting quaintness is no cure
Against the encroaching odours of the port,
Its failing apertures inhale the sea;
Besides, a wraith haunts there whom I know well,
Having created her in noon's despair.

Frail Donna of another century,
A grace of muslin, vineleaf and guitars,
She comes at noon, guarded by black duennas
To flute and bandol music from the bars,
Above the flies, molasses, donkey carts,
Above the clash of voices from the pier
Of stevedores gambling over tepid beer,
And stands as mute as old embroidery
On an old fashioned cushion of the heart.

II

Why should she hide against the dirty lace
Which stirs so still, its drift is scarcely seen
From the hot street? Why is that haunted face,
Dim as an antique faun's, fin de siècle style,
Imprisoned in the grillwork's leafless green
Who can evoke Alhambras with a smile?

9

Assailed by memory, desire stirs;
Yet that white hand against a rose cheek sleeping
That to the idler makes a subtle sign
Becomes a pigeon from a dark coign sweeping
As the coarse odour from the street defers
Anticipation of dark cellared wine.

Albums of lost Alhambras, swaying cypresses,
Brooding, daggered Moors and fanfares from da Falla,
A sable papa munching his moustache,
The scented note, the fearful assignation:
'I must, I must go now . . .', sighing, she sweeps
Her jewelled laces up as bells
Shatter the crystal park. The dark
Duennas weep,
They know the true necessity of that sleep
That withers centuries or the virgin rose.
Jesu Maria, what nonsense . . . I suppose . . .

III

I stir to smell the male, malodorous sea.
Another trance of mine is moving water.
How would it end? A merchant claims the daughter,
A man who hawks and profits in this heat,
Jeering at poets with a goldtoothed curse.
Girl, you were wise, whoever lived by verse?
The future is in cheap enamel wares.

Yet, Doña Maria, like a worn-out song
That keeps a phrase of wisdom in our ears,
Like the sad gaiety of a drunk guitar,
Like the bright gardens which blind vendors sell,
I watch your ancient, simple spirit where
Its letters flake across the balcony
From the façade of a third-rate hotel.

A Lesson for this Sunday

(postlapsarian eve?)

The growing idleness of summer grass
With its frail kites of furious butterflies
Requests the lemonade of simple praise
In scansion gentler than my hammock swings
And rituals no more upsetting than a
Black maid shaking linen as she sings
The plain notes of some protestant hosanna
Since I lie idling from the thought in things,

Or so they should. Until I hear the cries
Of two small children hunting yellow wings,
Who break my sabbath with the thought of sin.
Brother and sister, with a common pin,
Frowning like serious lepidopterists.
The little surgeon pierces the thin eyes.
Crouched on plump haunches, as a mantis prays
She shrieks to eviscerate its abdomen.
The lesson is the same. The maid removes
Both prodigies from their interest in science.
The girl, in lemon frock, begins to scream
As the maimed, teetering thing attempts its flight.
She is herself a thing of summery light,
Frail as a flower in this blue August air,
Not marked for some late grief that cannot speak.

The mind swings inward on itself in fear
Swayed towards nausea from each normal sign.
Heredity of cruelty everywhere,
And everywhere the frocks of summer torn,
The long look back to see where choice is born,
As summer grass sways to the scythe's design.

11

Allegre

Some mornings are as full of elation
As these pigeons crossing the hill slopes,
Silver as they veer in sunlight and white
On the warm blue shadows of the range.

And the sunward sides of the shacks
Gilded, as though this was Italy.

The bird's claws fasten round the lignum-vitae,
The roots of delight growing downward,
As the singer in his prime.

And the slopes of the forest this sunrise
Are thick with blue haze, as the colour
Of the woodsmoke from the first workman's fire.
A morning for wild bees and briersmoke,
For hands cupped to boys' mouths, the holloa
Of their cries in the cup of the valley.

The stream keeps its edges, wind-honed,
As the intellect is clear in affections,
Calm, with the rivulet's diligence.

Men are sawing with the wind on those ridges,
Trees arching, campeche, gommiers, canoe-wood,
The sawn trunks trundled down hillsides
To crash to the edge of the sea.
No temples, yet the fruits of intelligence,
No roots, yet the flowers of identity,
No cities, but white seas in sunlight,
Laughter and doves, like young Italy.

'Yet to find the true self is still arduous,
And for us, especially, the elation can be useless and empty
As this pale, blue ewer of the sky,
Loveliest in drought.

Conqueror

'March of Triumph'

This bronze, praised flayer of horses, who bred
Direction not valour in armies, has halted
On the crest of a ridge, in drizzling light;
His scaled gloves at rest
On the pommels, the wet-metal blaze
Of the sun in his sunken eye,
At the still, directionless hour
Of a changing, dragonish sky.

Iron deliverer whom the furies choose!
Half-human and half-deity in repose,
Envying each victim as its ravening grows,
Aye, the invincible! but whose
Armour cages a sigh no slaughter can depose.

Below him a thin harvest rusts in rain,
Lean flocks come limping to the herder's fife.
In that brown light, a mounted traveller
Splashes a silver river scarcely flowing
Through banks of ageing poplars;
On those unconquered peaks, it may be snowing.
On amber landscapes, hardly true to life

Is laid sometimes the quiet of unknowing
That elsewhere murderous teeth champ and devour,
As if such art placated nature's laws.
The small furred beast, spent beyond trembling
Contains such peace between its torturer's claws.

Take these small sparrows, witless if you will
That in the frightful glory of this hour
Flirt with that armed mass quiet on the hill,
Who dip, twitter, alight
On windless pennons, on these iron sheaves;

What are they? Fables of innocence trusting in power,
Or natural thoughts that haunt their source still?
If one cried out pity might shake the mind
Like a limp pennon in a sudden wind,
And joy remembered make rage the more.
And at that cry, the god must raise his hand
However wearily, and all respite end
In noise and neighing thunder, in a wealth
Of sounding brass and the conqueror, sighing descend
Down to the desolation of self.

Selections from

The Castaway

The Castaway

The starved eye devours the seascape for the morsel
Of a sail.

The horizon threads it infinitely.

Action breeds frenzy. I lie,
Sailing the ribbed shadow of a palm,
Afraid lest my own footprints multiply.

Blowing sand, thin as smoke,
Bored, shifts its dunes.
The surf tires of its castles like a child.

The salt green vine with yellow trumpet-flower,
A net, inches across nothing.
Nothing: the rage with which the sandfly's head is filled.

Pleasures of an old man:
Morning: contemplative evacuation, considering
The dried leaf, nature's plan.

In the sun, the dog's faeces
Crusts, whitens like coral.
We end in earth, from earth began.
In our own entrails, genesis.

If I listen I can hear the polyp build,
The silence thwanged by two waves of the sea.
Cracking a sea-louse, I make thunder split.

Godlike, annihilating godhead, art
And self, I abandon
Dead metaphors: the almond's leaf-like heart,

The ripe brain rotting like a yellow nut
Hatching
Its babel of sea-lice, sandfly and maggot,

That green wine bottle's gospel choked with sand,
Labelled, a wrecked ship,
Clenched seaward nailed and white as a man's hand.

The Swamp

Gnawing the highway's edges, its black mouth
Hums quietly: 'Home, come home . . .'

Behind its viscous breath the very word 'growth'
Grows fungi, rot;
White mottling its root.

More dreaded
Than canebreak, quarry, or sun-shocked gully-bed
Its horrors held Hemingway's hero rooted
To sure, clear shallows.

It begins nothing. Limbo of cracker convicts, Negroes.
Its black mood
Each sunset takes a smear of your life's blood.

Fearful, original sinuosities! Each mangrove sapling
Serpentlike, its roots obscene
As a six-fingered hand,

17

Conceals within its clutch the mossbacked toad,
Toadstools, the potent ginger-lily,
Petals of blood,

The speckled vulva of the tiger-orchid;
Outlandish phalloi
Haunting the travellers of its one road.

Deep, deeper than sleep
Like death,
Too rich in its decrescence, too close of breath,

In the fast-filling night, note
How the last bird drinks darkness with its throat,
How the wild saplings slip

Backward to darkness, go black
With widening amnesia, take the edge
Of nothing to them slowly, merge

Limb, tongue and sinew into a knot
Like chaos, like the road
Ahead.

The Flock

The grip of winter tightening, its thinned
volleys of blue-wing teal and mallard fly
from the longbows of reeds bent by the wind,
arrows of yearning for our different sky.
A season's revolution hones their sense,
whose target is our tropic light, while I
awoke this sunrise to a violence

of images migrating from the mind.
Skeletal forest, a sepulchral knight
riding in silence at a black tarn's edge
hooves cannonading snow
in the white funeral of the year,
antlike across the forehead of an alp
in iron contradiction crouched
against those gusts that urge the mallards south.
Vizor'd with blind defiance of his quest,
its yearly divination of the spring.
I travel through such silence, making dark
symbols with this pen's print across snow,
measuring winter's augury by words
settling the branched mind like migrating birds,
and never question when they come or go.

The style, tension of motion and the dark,
inflexible direction of the world
as it revolves upon its centuries
with change of language, climate, customs, light,
with our own prepossession day by day
year after year with images of flight,
survive our condemnation and the sun's
exultant larks.
      The dark, impartial Arctic
whose glaciers encased the mastodon,
froze giant minds in marble attitudes
revolves with tireless, determined grace
upon an iron axle, though the seals
howl with inhuman cries across its ice
and pages of torn birds are blown across
whitening tundras like engulfing snow.

Till its annihilation may the mind
reflect its fixity through winter, tropic,
until that equinox when the clear eye

clouds, like a mirror, without contradiction,
greet the black wings that cross it as a blessing
like the high, whirring flock that flew across
the cold sky of this page when I began
this journey by the wintry flare of dawn,
flying by instinct to their secret places
both for their need and for my sense of season.

The Whale, His Bulwark

To praise the blue whale's crystal jet,
To write, 'O fountain!' honouring a spout
Provokes this curse:
      'The high are humbled yet'
From those who humble Godhead, beasthood, verse.

Once, the Lord raised this bulwark to our eyes,
Once, in our seas, whales threshed,
The harpooner was common. Once, I heard
Of a baleine beached up the Grenadines, fleshed
By derisive, antlike villagers: a prize
Reduced from majesty to pygmy-size.
Salt-crusted, mythological,
And dead.

The boy who told me couldn't believe his eyes,
And I believed him. When I was small
God and a foundered whale were possible.
Whales are rarer, God as invisible.
Yet, through His gift, I praise the unfathomable,
Though the boy may be dead, the praise unfashionable,
The tale apocryphal.

20

Missing the Sea

Something removed roars in the ears of this house,
Hangs its drapes windless, stuns mirrors
Till reflections lack substance.

Some sound like the gnashing of windmills ground
To a dead halt;
A deafening absence, a blow.

It hoops this valley, weighs this mountain,
Estranges gesture, pushes this pencil
Through a thick nothing now,

Freights cupboards with silence, folds sour laundry
Like the clothes of the dead left exactly
As the dead behaved by the beloved,

Incredulous, expecting occupancy.

The Almond Trees

There's nothing here
this early;
cold sand
cold churning ocean, the Atlantic,
no visible history,

except this stand
of twisted, coppery, sea-almond trees
their shining postures surely
bent as metal, and one

foam-haired, salt-grizzled fisherman,
his mongrel growling, whirling on the stick
he pitches him; its spinning rays
'no visible history'
until their lengthened shapes amaze the sun.

By noon,
this further shore of Africa is strewn
with the forked limbs of girls toasting their flesh
in scarves, sunglasses, Pompeian bikinis,

brown daphnes, laurels, they'll all have
like their originals, their sacred grove,
this frieze
of twisted, coppery, sea-almond trees.

The fierce acetylene air
has singed
their writhing trunks with rust, the same
hues as a foundered, peeling barge.
It'll sear a pale skin copper with its flame.

The sand's white-hot ash underheel,
but their aged limbs have got their brazen sheen
from fire. Their bodies fiercely shine!
They're cured,
they endure their furnace.

Aged trees and oiled limbs share a common colour!

22

Welded in one flame,
huddling naked, stripped of their name,
for Greek or Roman tags, they were lashed
raw by wind, washed
out with salt and fire-dried,
bitterly nourished where their branches died,

their leaves' broad dialect a coarse,
enduring sound
they shared together.

Not as some running hamadryad's cries
rooted, broke slowly into leaf
her nipples peaking to smooth, wooden boles

Their grief
howls seaward through charred, ravaged holes.

One sunburnt body now acknowledges
that past and its own metamorphosis
as, moving from the sun, she kneels to spread
her wrap within the bent arms of this grove
that grieves in silence, like parental love.

Veranda

(for Ronald Bryden)

Grey apparitions at veranda ends
like smoke, divisible, but one
your age is ashes, its coherence gone,

Planters whose tears were marketable gum, whose voices
scratch the twilight like dried fronds
edged with reflection,

Colonels, hard as the commonwealth's greenheart,
middlemen, usurers whose art
kept an empire in the red,

Upholders of Victoria's china seas
lapping embossed around a drinking mug,
bully-boy roarers of the Empire club,

To the tarantara of the bugler, the sunset furled
round the last post,
the 'flamingo colours' of a fading world,

A ghost steps from you, my grandfather's ghost!
Uprooted from some rainy English shire,
you sought your Roman

End in suicide by fire.
Your mixed son gathered your charred, blackened bones,
in a child's coffin.

And buried them himself on a strange coast.
Sire,
why do I raise you up? Because

Your house has voices, your burnt house,
shrills with unguessed, lovely inheritors,
your genealogical roof tree, fallen, survives,
like seasoned timber through green, little lives.

I ripen towards your twilight, sir, that dream
where I am singed in that sea-crossing, steam
towards that vaporous world, whose souls,

like pressured trees brought diamonds out of coals.
The sparks pitched from your burning house are stars.
I am the man my father loved and was.

Whatever love you suffered makes amends
within them, father.
I climb the stair

And stretch a darkening hand to greet those friends
who share with you the last inheritance
of earth, our shrine and pardoner,

grey, ghostly loungers at veranda ends.

Lampfall

Closest at lampfall
Like children, like the moth-flame metaphor,
The Coleman's humming jet at the sea's edge
A tuning fork for our still family choir
Like Joseph Wright of Derby's astrological lecture
Casts rings of benediction round the aged.
I never tire of ocean's quarrelling,
Its silence, its raw voice,
Nor of these half-lit, windy leaves, gesticulating higher
'Rejoice, rejoice . . .'

But there's an old fish, a monster
Of primal fiction that drives barrelling
Undersea, too old to make a splash,
To which I'm hooked!

Through daydream, through nightmare trolling
Me so deep that no lights flash
There but the plankton's drifting, phosphorescent stars.

I see with its aged eyes,
Its dead green, glaucous gaze,
And I'm elsewhere, far as
I shall ever be from you whom I behold now
Dear family, dear friends, by this still glow,
The lantern's ring that the sea's
Never extinguished.
Your voices curl in the shell of my ear.

All day you've watched
The sea-rock like a loom
Shuttling its white wool, sheer Penelope!
The coals lit, the sky glows, an oven.
Heart into heart carefully laid
Like bread.
This is the fire that draws us by our dread
Of loss, the furnace door of heaven.

At night we have heard
The forest, an ocean of leaves, drowning her children,
Still, we belong here. There's Venus. We are not yet lost.

Like you, I preferred
The firefly's starlike little
Lamp, mining, a question,
to the highway's brightly multiplying beetles.

Selections from

The Gulf

Ebb

Year round, year round, we'll ride
this treadmill whose frayed tide
fretted with mud

leaves our suburban shoreline littered
with rainbow muck, the afterbirth
of industry, past scurf-

streaked bungalows
and pioneer factory;
but, blessedly, it narrows

through a dark aisle
of fountaining, gold coconuts, an oasis
marked for the yellow Caterpillar tractor.

We'll watch this shovelled too, but as we file
through its swift-wickered shade there always is
some island schooner netted in its weave

like a lamed heron
an oil-crippled gull;
a few more yards upshore

and it heaves free,
it races the horizon
with us, railed to one law,

ruled, like the washed-up moon
to circle her lost zone,
her radiance thinned.

The palm fronds signal wildly in the wind,
but we are bound elsewhere,
from the last sacred wood.

The schooner's out too far,
too far that boyhood.
Sometimes I turn to see

the schooner, crippled, try to tread the air,
the moon break in sere sail,
but without envy.

For safety, each sunfall,
the wildest of us all
mortgages life to fear.

And why not? From this car
there's terror enough in the habitual,
miracle enough in the familiar. Sure . . .

Hawk

(for Oliver Jackman)

Leaves shudder the drizzle's shine
like a treng-ka-treng from the cuatros,
beads fly from the tension line.
Gabilan, ay, gabilan,
high shadow, pitiless!
The old men without teeth,
rum-guzzlers, country fiddlers,

their rum-heads golden lakes
of a fabulous Yucatan,
Gabilan, ay, gabilan!

Caribs, like toothless tigers;
talons raking, a flash,
arrows like twanging wires,
catgut and ocelot,
merciless, that is man,
Gabilan, eh, gabilan?
Arima to Sangre Grande,
your wings like extended hands,
a grandee waltzing alone,
alone, to the old parang.

Gabilan, ay, gabilan,
the negroes, bastards, mestizos,
proud of their Spanish blood,
of the flesh, dripping like wires,
praising your hook, gabilan.
Above their slack mouths the hawk
floats tautly out of the cedars,
leaves the limbs shaking.

Slaves yearn for their master's talons,
the spur and the cold, gold eyes,
for the whips, whistling like wires,
time for our turn, gabilan!
But this hawk above Rampanalgas
rasps the sea with raw cries.
Hawks have no music.

Mass Man

Through a great lion's head clouded by mange
a black clerk growls.
Next, a gold-wired peacock withholds a man,
a fan, flaunting its oval, jewelled eyes;
What metaphors!
What coruscating, mincing fantasies!

Hector Mannix, water-works clerk, San Juan, has entered a
lion,
Boysie, two golden mangoes bobbing for breastplates, barges
like Cleopatra down her river, making style.
'Join us,' they shout, 'O God, child, you can't dance?'
But somewhere in that whirlwind's radiance
a child, rigged like a bat, collapses, sobbing.

But I am dancing, look, from an old gibbet
my bull-whipped body swings, a metronome!
Like a fruit-bat dropped in the silk-cotton's shade,
my mania, my mania is a terrible calm.

Upon your penitential morning,
some skull must rub its memory with ashes,
some mind must squat down howling in your dust,
some hand must crawl and recollect your rubbish,
someone must write your poems.

Landfall, Grenada

(for Robert Head, Mariner)

Where you are rigidly anchored,
the groundswell of blue foothills, the blown canes
surging to cumuli cannot be heard;
like the slow, seamless ocean,
one motion folds the grass where you were lowered,
and the tiered sea
whose grandeurs you detested
climbs out of sound.

Its moods held no mythology
for you, it was a working-place
of tonnage and ruled stars;
you chose your landfall with a mariner's
casual certainty,
calm as that race
into whose heart you harboured;
your death was a log's entry,
your suffering held the strenuous
reticence of those
whose rites are never public,
hating to impose, to offend.
Deep friend, teach me to learn
such ease, such landfall going,
such mocking tolerance of those
neat, gravestone elegies
that rhyme our end.

Homecoming: Anse La Raye

(for Garth St Omer)

Whatever else we learned
at school, like solemn Afro-Greeks eager for grades,
of Helen and the shades
of borrowed ancestors,
there are no rites
for those who have returned,
only, when her looms fade,
drilled in our skulls, the doom-
surge-haunted nights,
only this well-known passage
under the coconuts' salt-rusted
swords, these rotted
leathery sea-grapes leaves,
the seacrabs' brittle helmets, and
this barbecue of branches, like the ribs
of sacrificial oxen on scorched sand;
only this fish-gut reeking beach
whose spindly, sugar-headed children race
whose starved, pot-bellied children race
pelting up from the shallows
because your clothes,
your posture
seem a tourist's.
They swarm like flies
round your heart's sore.

Suffer them to come,
entering your needle's eye,
knowing whether they live or die,

33

what others make of life will pass them by
like that far silvery freighter
threading the horizon like a toy;
for once, like them,
you wanted no career
but this sheer light, this clear,
infinite, boring, paradisal sea,
but hoped it would mean something to declare
today, I am your poet, yours,
all this you knew,
but never guessed you'd come
to know there are homecomings without home.

You give them nothing.
Their curses melt in air.
The black cliffs scowl,
the ocean sucks its teeth,
like that dugout canoe
a drifting petal fallen in a cup,
with nothing but its image,
you sway, reflecting nothing.
The freighter's silvery ghost
is gone, the children gone.
Dazed by the sun
you trudge back to the village
past the white, salty esplanade
under whose palms, dead
fishermen move their draughts in shade,
crossing, eating their islands,
and one, with a politician's
ignorant, sweet smile, nods,
as if all fate
swayed in his lifted hand.

Cold Spring Harbour

From feather-stuffed bolsters of cloud
falling on casual linen
the small shrieks soundlessly float.
The woods are lint-wreathed. Dawn
crackles like foil to the rake
of a field mouse nibbling, nibbling
its icing. The world is unwrapped
in cotton and you would tread wool
if you opened, quietly, whitely,
this door, like an old Christmas card
turned by a child's dark hand, did
he know it was dark then,
the magical brittle branches, the white house
collared in fur, the white world of men,
its bleeding gules and its berry drops?

Two prancing, immobile white ponies
no bigger than mice pulled a carriage
across soundless hillocks of cotton;
bells hasped to their necks didn't tinkle
though you begged God to touch them to life,
some white-haired old God who'd forgotten
or no longer trusted his miracles.
What urges you now towards this white,
snow-whipped wood is not memory
of that dark child's toys, not the card
of a season, forever foreign, that went
over its ridges like a silent
sleigh. That was a child's sorrow, this is
child's play, through which you cannot go,
dumbstruck at an open door,

stunned, fearing the strange violation
(because you are missing your children)
of perfect snow.

Love in the Valley

The sun goes slowly blind.
It is this mountain, shrouding
the valley of the shadow,

widening like amnesia
evening dims the mind.
I shake my head in darkness,

it is a tree branched with cries,
a trash-can full of print.
Now, through the reddening squint

of leaves leaden as eyes,
a skein of drifting hair
like a twig, fallen on snow,

branches the blank pages.
I bring it close, and stare
in slow vertiginous darkness,

and now I drift elsewhere,
through hostile images
of white and black, and look,

like a thaw-sniffing stallion, the head
of Pasternak emerges with its forelock,
his sinewy wrist a fetlock

pawing the frozen spring,
till his own hand has frozen
on the white page, heavy.

I ride through a white childhood
whose pines glittered with bracelets,
when I heard wolves, feared the black wood,

every wrist-aching brook
and the ice maiden
in Hawthorne's fairy book.

The hair melts into dark,
a question mark that led
where the untethered mind

strayed from its first track;
now Hardy's sombre head
upon which hailstorms broke

looms, like a weeping rock,
like wind, the tresses drift
and their familiar trace

tingles across the face
with light lashes.
I knew the depth of whiteness,

I feared the numbing kiss
of those women of winter,
Bathsheba, Lara, Tess,

whose tragedy made less
of life, whose love was more
than love of literature.

Nearing Forty

(for John Figueroa)

The irregular combination of fanciful invention may
delight awhile by that novelty of which the common
satiety of life sends us all in quest. But the pleasures of
sudden wonder are soon exhausted and the mind can
only repose on the stability of truth . . .

SAMUEL JOHNSON

Insomniac since four, hearing this narrow,
rigidly-metred, early-rising rain
recounting, as its coolness numbs the marrow,
that I am nearing forty, nearer the weak
vision thickening to a frosted pane,
nearer the day when I may judge my work
by the bleak modesty of middle-age
as a false dawn, fireless and average,
which would be just, because your life bled for
the household truth, the style past metaphor
that finds its parallel however wretched
in simple, shining lines, in pages stretched
plain as a bleaching bedsheet under a gutter-
ing rainspout, glad for the sputter
of occasional insight; you who foresaw
ambition as a searing meteor
will fumble a damp match, and smiling, settle

38

for the dry wheezing of a dented kettle,
for vision narrower than a louvre's gap,
then watching your leaves thin, recall how deep
prodigious cynicism plants its seed,
gauges our seasons by this year's end rain
which, as greenhorns at school, we'd
call conventional for convectional;
or you will rise and set your lines to work
with sadder joy but steadier elation,
until the night when you can really sleep,
measuring how imagination
ebbs, conventional as any water-clerk
who weighs the force of lightly-falling rain,
which, as the new moon moves it, does its work,
even when it seems to weep.

The Walk

After hard rain the eaves repeat their beads,
those trees exhale your doubt like mantled tapers,
drop after drop, like a child's abacus
beads of cold sweat file from high tension wires,

pray for us, pray for this house, borrow your neighbour's
faith, pray for this brain that tires,
and loses faith in the great books it reads;
after a day spent prone, haemorrhaging poems,

each phrase peeled from the flesh in bandages,
arise, stroll on under a sky
sodden as kitchen laundry,

while the cats yawn behind their window frames,
lions in cages of their choice,
no further though, than your last neighbour's gates
figured with pearl. How terrible is your own

fidelity, O heart, O rose of iron!
When was your work more like a housemaid's novel,
some drenched soap-opera which gets
closer than yours to life? Only the pain,

the pain is real. Here's your life's end,
a clump of bamboos whose clenched
fist loosens its flowers, a track
that hisses through the rain-drenched

grove: abandon all, the work,
the pain of a short life. Startled, you move;
your house, a lion rising, paws you back.

Selections from

Another Life

Extract A:

CHAPTER 1

i

Verandahs, where the pages of the sea
are a book left open by an absent master
in the middle of another life—
I begin here again,
begin until this ocean's
a shut book, and, like a bulb
the white moon's filaments wane.

Begin with twilight, when a glare
which held a cry of bugles lowered
the coconut lances of the inlet,
as a sun, tired of empire, declined.
It mesmerized like fire without wind,
and as its amber climbed
the beer-stein ovals of the British fort
above the promontory, the sky
grew drunk with light.
                              There
was your heaven! The clear
glaze of another life,
a landscape locked in amber, the rare
gleam. The dream
of reason had produced its monster:
a prodigy of the wrong age and colour.

All afternoon the student
with the dry fever of some draughtsman's clerk
had magnified the harbour, now twilight

eager to complete itself,
drew a girl's figure to the open door
of a stone boathouse with a single stroke, then fell
to a reflecting silence. This silence waited
for the verification of detail:
the gables of the Saint Antoine Hotel
aspiring from jungle, the flag
at Government House melting its pole,
and for the tidal amber glare to glaze
the last shacks of the Morne till they became
transfigured sheerly by the student's will,
a cinquecento fragment in gilt frame.

The vision died,
the black hills simplified
to hunks of coal,
but if the light was dying through the stone
of that converted boathouse on the pier,
a girl, blowing its embers in her kitchen,
could feel its epoch entering her hair.

Darkness, soft as amnesia, furred the slope.
He rose and climbed towards the studio.
The last hill burned,
the sea crinkled like foil,
a moon ballooned up from the Wireless Station. O
mirror, where a generation yearned
for whiteness, for candour, unreturned.

The moon maintained her station,
her fingers stroked a chiton-fluted sea,
her disc whitewashed the shells
of gutted offices barnacling the wharves
of the burnt town, her lamp
baring the ovals of toothless façades,
along the Roman arches, as he passed

her alternating ivories lay untuned,
her age was dead, her sheet
shrouded the antique furniture, the mantel
with its plaster-of-Paris Venus, which
his yearning had made marble, half-cracked
unsilvering mirror of black servants,
like the painter's kerchiefed, ear-ringed portrait: Albertina.

Within the door, a bulb
haloed the tonsure of a reader crouched
in its pale tissue like an embryo,
the leisured gaze
turned towards him, the short arms
yawned briefly, welcome. Let us see.
Brown, balding, a lacertilian
jut to its underlip,
with spectacles thick as a glass paperweight
over eyes the hue of the sea-smoothed bottle glass,
the man wafted the drawing to his face
as if dusk were myopic, not his gaze.
Then, with slow strokes the master changed the sketch.

Extract B:

CHAPTER 1

iii

They sang, against the rasp and cough of shovels,
against the fists of mud pounding the coffin,
the diggers' wrists rounding off every phrase,
their iron hymn, 'The Pilgrims of the Night'.

In the sea-dusk, the live child waited
for the other to escape, a flute
of frail, seraphic mist,
but their black, Bible-paper voices fluttered shut, silence
re-entered every mould, it wrapped the edges
of sea-eaten stone, mantled the blind
eternally gesturing angels, strengthened the flowers
with a different patience, and left
or lost its hoarse voice in the shells
that trumpeted from the graves. The world
stopped swaying and settled in its place.
A black lace glove swallowed his hand.
The engine of the sea began again.

A night-black hearse, tasselled and heavy, lugged
an evening of blue smoke across the field,
like an old wreath the mourners broke apart
and drooped like flowers over the streaked stones
deciphering dates. The gravekeeper with his lantern-jaw
(years later every lantern-swinging porter
guarding infinite rails repeated this), opened
the yellow doorway to his lodge. Wayfarer's station.
The child's journey was signed.
The ledger drank its entry.
Outside the cemetery gates life stretched from sleep.
Gone to her harvest of flax-headed angels,
of seraphs blowing pink-palated conchs,
gone, so they sang, into another light:
But was it her?
Or Thomas Alva Lawrence's dead child,
another Pinkie, in her rose gown floating?
Both held the same dark eyes,
slow, haunting coals, the same curved
ivory hand touching the breast,
as if, answering death, each whispered 'Me?'

Extract C:

CHAPTER 7

i

Provincialism loves the pseudo-epic,
so if these heroes have been given a stature
disproportionate to their cramped lives,
remember I beheld them at knee-height,
and that their thunderous exchanges
rumbled like gods about another life,
as now, I hope, some child
ascribes their grandeur to Gregorias.
Remember years must pass before he saw an orchestra,
a train, a theatre, the spark-coloured leaves
of autumn whirling from a rail-line,
that, as for the seasons,
the works he read described their passage with
processional arrogance; then pardon, life,
if he saw autumn in a rusted leaf.
What else was he but a divided child?

I saw, as through the glass of some provincial gallery
the hieratic objects which my father loved:
the stuffed dark nightingale of Keats,
bead-eyed, snow-headed eagles,
all that romantic taxidermy,
and each one was a fragment of the True Cross,
each one upheld, as if it were The Host;
those venerated, venerable objects
borne by the black hands (reflecting like mahogany)
of reverential teachers, shone the more
they were repolished by our use.

The Church upheld the Word, but this new Word
was here, attainable
to my own hand,
in the deep country it found the natural man,
generous, rooted.
And I now yearned to suffer for that life,
I looked for some ancestral, tribal country,
I heard its clear tongue over the clean stones
of the river, I looked from the bus-window
and multiplied the bush with savages,
speckled the leaves with jaguar and deer,
I changed those crusted boulders
to grey, stone-lidded crocodiles,
my head shrieked with metallic, raucous parrots,
I held my breath as savages grinned,
stalking, through the bush.

ii

About the August of my fourteenth year
I lost my self somewhere above a valley
owned by a spinster-farmer, my dead father's friend.
At the hill's edge there was a scarp
with bushes and boulders stuck in its side.
Afternoon light ripened the valley,
rifling smoke climbed from small labourers' houses,
and I dissolved into a trance.

I was seized by a pity more profound
than my young body could bear, I climbed
with the labouring smoke,
I drowned in labouring breakers of bright cloud,
then uncontrollably I began to weep,
inwardly, without tears, with a serene extinction

47

of all sense; I felt compelled to kneel,
I wept for nothing and for everything,
I wept for the earth of the hill under my knees,
for the grass, the pebbles, for the cooking smoke
above the labourers' houses like a cry,
for unheard avalanches of white cloud,
but 'darker grows the valley, more and more forgetting'.
For their lights still shine through the hovels like litmus,
the smoking lamp still slowly says its prayer,
the poor still move behind their tinted scrim,
the taste of water is still shared everywhere,
but in that ship of night, locked in together,
through which, like chains, a little light might leak,
something still fastens us forever to the poor.

But which was the true light?
Blare noon or twilight,
'the lonely light that Samuel Palmer engraved',
or the cold
iron entering the soul, as the soul sank
out of belief.
           That bugle-coloured twilight
blew the withdrawal not of legions and proconsuls,
but of pale, prebendary clerks, with the gait and gall
of camels. And yet I envied them,
bent, silent decipherers of sacred texts,
their Roman arches, Vergilian terraces,
their tiered, ordered colonial world
where evening, like the talons of a bird
bent the blue jacaranda softly, and smoke rose with
the leisure and frailty of recollection,
I learnt their strict necrology of dead kings,
bones freckling the rushes of damp tombs,
the light-furred luminous world of Claude,
their ruined temples, and in drizzling twilights, Turner.

iii

Our father,
	who floated in the vaults of Michelangelo,
Saint Raphael,
	of sienna and gold leaf,
it was then
	that he fell in love, having no care
for truth,
	that he could enter the doorway of a triptych,
that he believed
	those three stiff horsemen cantering past a rock,
	towards jewelled cities on a cracked horizon,
	that the lances of Uccello shivered him,
	like Saul, unhorsed,
that he fell in love with art,
	and life began.

iv

Noon,
	and its sacred water sprinkles.
A schoolgirl in blue and white uniform,
her golden plaits a simple coronet
out of Angelico, a fine sweat on her forehead,
hair where the twilight singed and signed its epoch.
And a young man going home.
They move away from each other.
They are moving towards each other.
His head roars with hunger and poems.
His hand is trembling to recite her name.
She clutches her books, she is laughing,
her uniformed companions laughing.
She laughs till she is near tears.

Who could tell, in 'the crossing of that pair'
        that later it would mean
that rigid iron lines were drawn between
        him and that garden chair
from which she rose to greet him, as for a train,
        that watching her rise
from the bright boathouse door was like some station
        where either stood, transfixed
by the rattling telegraph of carriage windows
        flashing goodbyes,
that every dusk rehearsed a separation
        already in their eyes,
that later, when they sat in silence, seaward,
        and looking upward, heard
its engines as some moonlit liner chirred
        from the black harbour outward,
those lights spelt out their sentence, word by word?

Extract D:

from CHAPTER 8

i

Around that golden year which I described
Gregorias and that finished soldier quartered
in a brown, broken-down bungalow
whose yard was indistinguishable from bush,
between the broad-leaved jungle and the town.
Shaky, half-rotted treaders, sighing, climbed
towards a sun-warped verandah, one half of which
Gregorias had screened into a studio,

shading a varnished, three-legged table
crawling with exhausted paint-tubes, a lowering quart
of *Pirate* rum, and grey, dog-eared, turpentine-stained editions
of the Old Masters. One day the floor collapsed.
The old soldier sank suddenly to his waist
wearing the verandah like a belt.
Gregorias buckled with laughter telling this,
but shame broke the old warrior.
The dusk lowered his lances through the leaves.
In another year the soldier shrank and died.
Embittered, Gregorias wanted carved on his stone:
PRAISE YOUR GOD, DRINK YOUR RUM, MIND YOUR OWN BUSINESS.

We were both fatherless now, and often drunk.

Drunk,
            on a half-pint of joiner's turpentine,
drunk,
            while the black, black-sweatered, horn-soled fisher-
                men drank
            their *l'absinthe* in sand back yards standing up,
            on the clear beer of sunrise,
            on cheap, tannic Canaries muscatel,
            on glue, on linseed oil, on kerosene,
            as Van Gogh's shadow rippling on a cornfield,
            on Cézanne's boots grinding the stones of Aix
            to shales of slate, ochre and Vigie blue,
            on Gauguin's hand shaking the gin-coloured dew
            from the umbrella yams,
            garrulous, all day, sun-struck,
till dusk glazed vision with its darkening varnish.
Days welded by the sun's torch into days!
Gregorias plunging whole-suit in the shallows,
painting under water, roaring, and spewing spray,
Gregorias gesturing, under the coconuts
wickerwork shade-tin glare-wickerwork shade.

days woven into days, a stinging haze
of thorn trees bent like green flames by the Trades,
under a sky tacked to the horizon, drumskin tight,
as shaggy combers leisurely beard the rocks,
while the asphalt sweats its mirages and the beaks
of fledgling ginger lilies
gasped for rain.
Gregorias, the easel rifled on his shoulder, marching
towards an Atlantic flashing tinfoil,
singing 'O Paradiso',
till the western breakers laboured to that music,
his canvas crucified against a tree.

ii

But drunkenly, or secretly, we swore,
disciples of that astigmatic saint,
that we would never leave the island
until we had put down, in paint, in words,
as palmists learn the network of a hand,
all of its sunken, leaf-choked ravines,
every neglected, self-pitying inlet
muttering in brackish dialect, the ropes of mangroves
from which old soldier crabs slipped
surrendering to slush,
each ochre track seeking some hilltop and
losing itself in an unfinished phrase,
under sand shipyards where the burnt-out palms
inverted the design of unrigged schooners,
entering forests, boiling with life,
goyave, corrosol, bois-canot, sapotille.

Days!
The sun drumming, drumming,
past the defeated pennons of the palms,
roads limp from sunstroke,

past green flutes of grass
the ocean cannonading, come!
Wonder that opened like the fan
of the dividing fronds
on some noon-struck Sahara,
where my heart from its rib-cage yelped like a pup
after clouds of sanderlings rustily wheeling
the world on its ancient,
invisible axis,
the breakers slow-dolphining over more breakers,
to swivel our easels down, as firm
as conquerors who had discovered home.

Extract E:

CHAPTER 12

iv

And how could we know then,
damned poet and damned painter,
that we too would resemble
those nervous, inflamed men,
fisherman and joiner,
with their quivering addiction
to alcohol and failure,
who hover in a fiction
of flaming palely at doors
for the rumshop lamp to glare,
with watered eyes, loose collars
and the badge of a bone stud,
their vision branched with blood,

their bodies trees which fed
a fire beyond control,
drinkers who lost their pride
when pride in drink was lost.
We saw, within their eyes,
we thought, an artist's ghost,
but dignified, dignified
through days eaten with shame;
we were burned out that year
with the old sacred flame,
we swore to make drink
and art our finishing school,
join brush and pen and name
to the joiner's strenuous tool.

And then, one night, somewhere,
a single outcry rocketed in air,
the thick tongue of a fallen, drunken lamp
licked at its alcohol ringing the floor,
and with the fierce rush of a furnace door
suddenly opened, history was here.

Extract F:

CHAPTER 14

—*Anna awaking*

When the oil green water glows but doesn't catch,
only its burnish, something wakes me early,
draws me out breezily to the pebbly shelf
of shallows where the water chuckles
and the ribbed boats sleep like children,

buoyed on their creases. I have nothing to do,
the burnished kettle is already polished,
to see my own blush burn,
and the last thing the breeze needs is my exhilaration.

I lie to my body with useless chores.
The ducks, if they ever slept, waddle knowingly.
The pleats of the shallows are neatly creased
and decorous and processional,
they arrive at our own harbour from the old Hospital
across the harbour. When the first canoe,
silent, will not wave at me,
I understand, we are acknowledging
our separate silences, as the one silence,
I know that they know my peace as I know theirs.
I am amazed that the wind is tirelessly fresh.
The wind is older than the world.

It is always one thing at a time.
Now, it is always girlish.
I am happy enough to see it as a kind
of dimpled, impish smiling.
When the sleep-smelling house stirs
to that hoarse first cough, that child's first cry,
that rumbled, cavernous questioning of my mother,
I come out of the cave
like the wind emerging,
like a bride, to her first morning.

I shall make coffee.
The light, like a fiercer dawn,
will singe the downy edges of my hair,
and the heat will plate my forehead till it shines.
Its sweat will share the excitement of my cunning.
Mother, I am in love.
Harbour, I am waking.

I know the pain in your budding, nippled limes,
I know why your limbs shake, windless, pliant trees.
I shall grow grey as this light.
The first flush will pass.
But there will always be morning,
and I shall have this fever waken me,
whoever I lie to, lying close to, sleeping
like a ribbed boat in the last shallows of night.

But even if I love not him but the world,
and the wonder of the world in him, of him in the world,
and the wonder that he makes the world waken to me,
I shall never grow old in him,
I shall always be morning to him,
and I must walk and be gentle as morning.
Without knowing it, like the wind,
that cannot see her face,
the serene humility of her exultation,
that having straightened the silk sea smooth, having noticed
that the comical ducks ignore her, that
the childish pleats of the shallows are set straight,
that everyone, even the old, sleeps in innocence,
goes in nothing, naked, as I would be,
if I had her nakedness, her transparent body.
The bells garland my head. I could be happy,
just because today is Sunday. No, for more.

ii

Then Sundays, smiling, carried in both hands
a towelled dish bubbling with the good life
whose fervour steaming, beaded her clear brow,
from which damp skeins were brushed,
and ladled out her fullness to the brim.
And all those faded prints that pressed their scent

56

on her soft, house-warm body,
glowed from her flesh with work,
her hands that held the burnish of dry hillsides
freckled with fire-light,
hours that ripened till the fullest hour
could burst with peace.

'Let's go for a little walk,' she said, one afternoon,
'I'm in a walking mood.' Near the lagoon,
dark water's lens had made the trees one wood
arranged to frame this pair whose pace
unknowingly measured loss,
each face was set towards its character.
Where they now stood, others before had stood,
the same lens held them, the repeated wood,
then there grew on each one
the self-delighting, self-transfiguring stone
stare of the demi-god.
Stunned by their images they strolled on, content
that the black film of water kept the print
of their locked images when they passed on.

iii

And which of them in time would be betrayed
was never questioned by that poetry
which breathed within the evening naturally,
but by the noble treachery of art
that looks for fear when it is least afraid,
that coldly takes the pulse-beat of the heart
in happiness; that praised its need to die
to the bright candour of the evening sky,
that preferred love to immortality;
so every step increased that subtlety
which hoped that their two bodies could be made

one body of immortal metaphor.
The hand she held already had betrayed
them by its longing for describing her.

Extract G:

CHAPTER 15

i

Still dreamt of, still missed,
especially on raw, rainy mornings, your face shifts
into anonymous schoolgirl faces, a punishment,
since sometimes, you condescend to smile,
since at the corners of the smile there is forgiveness.

Besieged by sisters, you were a prize
of which they were too proud, circled
by the thorn thicket of their accusation,
what grave deep wrong, what wound have you brought Anna?

The rain season comes with its load.
The half-year has travelled far. Its back hurts.
It drizzles wearily.

It is twenty years since,
after another war, the shell-cases are where?
But in our brassy season, our imitation autumn,
your hair puts out its fire,
your gaze haunts innumerable photographs,

now clear, now indistinct,
all that pursuing generality,
that vengeful conspiracy with nature,

all that sly informing of objects,
and behind every line, your laugh
frozen into a lifeless photograph.

In that hair I could walk through the wheatfields of Russia,
your arms were downed and ripening pears,
for you became, in fact, another country,

you are Anna of the wheatfield and the weir,
you are Anna of the solid winter rain,
Anna of the smoky platform and the cold train,
in that war of absence, Anna of the steaming stations,

gone from the marsh-edge,
from the drizzled shallows
puckering with gooseflesh,
Anna of the first green poems that startlingly hardened,

of the mellowing breasts now,
Anna of the lurching, long flamingos
of the harsh salt lingering in the thimble
of the bather's smile,

Anna of the darkened house, among the reeking shell-cases
lifting my hand and swearing us to her breast,
unbearably clear-eyed.

You are all Annas, enduring all goodbyes,
within the cynical station of your body,
Christie, Karenina, big-boned and passive,

that I found life within some novel's leaves
more real than you, already chosen
as his doomed heroine. You knew, you knew.

ii

Who were you, then?
The golden partisan of my young Revolution,
my braided, practical, seasoned commissar,

your back, bent at its tasks, in the blue kitchen,
or hanging flags of laundry, feeding the farm's chickens,
against a fantasy of birches,

poplars or whatever.
As if a pen's eye could catch that virginal litheness,
as if shade and sunlight leoparding the blank page
could be so literal,

foreign as snow,
far away as first love,
my Akhmatoval!

Twenty years later, in the odour of burnt shells,
you can remind me of 'A Visit to the Pasternaks',
so that you are suddenly the word 'wheat',

falling on the ear, against the frozen silence of a weir,
again you are bending
over a cabbage garden, tending
a snowdrift of rabbits,
or pulling down the clouds from the thrumming clotheslines.

If dreams are signs,
then something died this minute,
its breath blown from a different life,

from a dream of snow, from paper
to white paper flying, gulls and herons
following this plough. And now,

you are suddenly old, white-haired,
like the herons, the turned page. Anna, I wake
to the knowledge that things sunder
from themselves, like peeling bark,

to the emptiness
of a bright silence shining after thunder.

iii

'Any island would drive you crazy',
I knew you'd grow tired
of all that iconography of the sea

like the young wind, a bride
riffling daylong the ocean's catalogue
of shells and algae,

everything, this flock
of white, novitiate herons
I saw in the grass of a grey parish church,

like nurses, or young nuns after communion,
their sharp eyes sought me out
as yours once, only.

61

And you were heron-like,
a water-haunter,
you grew bored with your island,

till, finally, you took off,
without a cry,
a novice in your nurse's uniform,

years later I imagined you
walking through trees to some grey hospital,
serene communicant,
but never 'lonely',

like the wind, never to be married,
your faith like folded linen, a nun's, a nurse's,
why should you read this now?

No woman should read verses
twenty years late. You go about your calling, candle-like
carrying yourself down a dark aisle

of wounded, married to the sick,
knowing one husband, pain,
only with the heron-flock, the rain,

the stone church, I remembered . . .
Besides, the slender, virginal New Year's
just married, like a birch
to a few crystal tears,

and like a birch bent at the register
who cannot, for a light's flash, change her name,
she still writes '65 for '66;

so, watching the tacit
ministering herons, each at its
work among the dead, the stone church, the stones,

I made this in your honour, when
vows and affections failing
your soul leapt like a heron sailing
from the salt, island grass

into another heaven.

Extract H:

CHAPTER 20

iv

Well, there you have your seasons, prodigy!
For instance, the autumnal fall of bodies,
deaths, like a comic, brutal repetition,
and in the Book of Hours, that seemed so far,
the light and amber of another life,
there is a Reaper busy about his wheat,
one who stalks nearer, and will not look up
from the scythe's swish in the orange evening grass,

and the fly at the font of your ear
sings, Hurry, hurry!
Never to set eyes on this page,
ah Harry, never to read our names,
like a stone blurred with tears I could not read
among the pilgrims, and the mooning child
staring from the window of the high studio.

Brown, balding, with a lacertilian
jut to his underiip,
with spectacles thick as a glass paperweight
and squat, blunt fingers,
waspish, austere, swift with asperities,

with a dimpled pot for a belly from the red clay of Piaille.
Eyes like the glint of sea-smoothed bottle glass,
his knee-high khaki stockings,
brown shoes lacquered even in desolation.

People entered his understanding
like a wayside country church,
they had built him themselves.
It was they who had smoothed the wall
of his clay-coloured forehead,
who made of his rotundity an earthy
useful object
holding the clear water of their simple troubles,
he who returned their tribal names
to the adze, mattock, midden and cookingpot.

A tang of white rum on the tongue of the mandolin,
a young bay, parting its mouth,
a heron silently named or a night-moth,
or the names of villages plaited into one map,
in the evocation of scrubbed back-yard smoke,
and he is a man no more
but the fervour and intelligence
of a whole country.

Leonce, Placide, Alcindor,
Dominic, from whose plane vowels were shorn
odorous as forest,
ask the charcoal-burner to look up
with his singed eyes,
ask the lip-cracked fisherman three miles at sea
with nothing between him and Dahomey's coast
to dip rain-water over his parched boards
for Monsieur Simmons, *pour* Msieu Harry Simmons,
let the husker on his pyramid of coconuts
rest on his tree.

Blow out the eyes in the unfinished portraits.

And the old woman who danced
with a spine like the 'glory cedar',
so lissom that her veins bulged evenly
upon the tightened drumskin of the earth,
her feet nimbler than the drummer's fingers,
let her sit in her corner and become evening
for a man the colour of her earth,
for a cracked claypot full of idle brushes,
and the tubes curl and harden,
except the red,
except the virulent red!

His island forest, open and enclose him
like a rare butterfly between its leaves.

Extract I:

from CHAPTER 22

That child who sets his half-shell afloat
in the brown creek that is Rampanalgas River—
my son first, then two daughters—
towards the roar of waters,
towards the Atlantic with a dead almond leaf for a sail,
with a twig for a mast,
was, like his father, this child,
a child without history, without knowledge of its pre-world,

only the knowledge of water runnelling rocks,
and the desperate whelk that grips the rock's outcrop
like a man whom the waves can never wash overboard;
that child who puts the shell's howl to his ear,
hears nothing, hears everything
that the historian cannot hear, the howls
of all the races that crossed the water,
the howls of grandfathers drowned
in that intricately swivelled Babel,
hears the fellaheen, the Madrasi, the Mandingo, the Ashanti,
yes, and hears also the echoing green fissures of Canton,
and thousands without longing for this other shore
by the mud tablets of the Indian Provinces,
robed ghostly white and brown, the twigs of uplifted hands,
of manacles, mantras, of a thousand kaddishes,
whorled, drilling into the shell,
see, in the evening light by the saffron, sacred Benares,
how they are lifting like herons,
robed ghostly white and brown,
and the crossing of water has erased their memories.
And the sea, which is always the same,
accepts them.
And the shore, which is always the same,
accepts them.

In the shallop of the shell,
in the round prayer,
in the palate of the conch,
in the dead sail of the almond leaf
are all of the voyages.

Extract J:

CHAPTER 23

iii

I looked from old verandas at
verandas, sails, the eternal summer sea
like a book left open by an absent master.
And what if it's all gone,
the hill's cut away for more tarmac,
the groves all sawn,
and bungalows proliferate on the scarred, hacked hillside,
the magical lagoon drained
for the Higher Purchase plan,
and they've bulldozed and bowdlerized our Vigie,
our *ocelle insularum*, our Sirmio
for a pink and pastel New Town where the shacks and huts
    stood
teetering and tough in unabashed unhope,
as twilight like amnesia blues the slope,
when over the untroubled ocean, the moon
will always swing its lantern
and evening fold the pages of the sea,
and peer like my lost reader silently
between the turning leaves
for the lost names
of Caribs, slaves and fishermen?

Forgive me, you folk,
who exercise a patience
subtler, stronger than the muscles
in the wave's wrist,
and you, sea, with the mouth
of that old gravekeeper

white-headed, lantern-jawed,
forgive our desertions, you islands
whose names dissolve like sugar
in a child's mouth. And you, Gregorias.
And you, Anna. Rest.

iv

But, ah Gregorias,
I christened you with that Greek name because
it echoes the blest thunders of the surf,
because you painted our first, primitive frescoes,
because it sounds explosive,
a black Greek's! A sun that stands back
from the fire of itself, not shamed, prizing
its shadow, watching it blaze!
You sometimes dance with that destructive frenzy
that made our years one fire.
Gregorias listen, lit,
we were the light of the world!
We were blest with a virginal, unpainted world
with Adam's task of giving things their names,
with the smooth white walls of clouds and villages
where you devised your inexhaustible,
impossible Renaissance,
brown cherubs of Giotto and Masaccio,
with the salt wind coming through the window,
smelling of turpentine, with nothing so old
that it could not be invented,
and set above it your crude wooden star,
its light compounded in that mortal glow:
Gregorias, Apilo!

April 1965 – April 1972

Selections from

Sea Grapes

The Virgins

Down the dead streets of sun-stoned Frederiksted,
the first freeport to die for tourism,
strolling at funeral pace, I am reminded
of life not lost to the American dream;
but my small-islander's simplicities
can't better our new empire's civilized
exchange of cameras, watches, perfumes, brandies
for the good life, so cheaply underpriced
that only the crime rate is on the rise
in streets blighted with sun, stone arches
and plazas blown dry by the hysteria
of rumour. A condominium drowns
in vacancy; its bargains are dusted,
but only a jewelled housefly drones
over the bargains. The roulettes spin
rustily to the wind; the vigorous trade
that every morning would begin afresh
by revving up green water round the pierhead
heading for where the banks of silver thresh.

Adam's Song

The adulteress stoned to death,
is killed in our own time
by whispers, by the breath
that films her flesh with slime.

70

The first was Eve,
who horned God for the serpent,
for Adam's sake; which makes
everyone guilty or Eve innocent.

Nothing has changed
for men still sing the song that Adam sang
against the world he lost to vipers,

the song to Eve
against his own damnation;
he sang it in the evening of the world

with the lights coming on in the eyes
of panthers in the peaceable kingdom
and his death coming out of the trees,

he sings it, frightened
of the jealousy of God and at the price
of his own death.

The song ascends to God, who wipes his eyes:

'Heart, you are in my heart as the bird rises,
heart, you are in my heart while the sun sleeps,
heart, you lie still in me as the dew is,
you weep within me, as the rain weeps.'

Parades, Parades

There's the wide desert, but no one marches
except in the pads of old caravans,
there is the ocean, but the keels incise
the precise, old parallels,
there's the blue sea above the mountains
but they scratch the same lines
in the jet trails –
so the politicians plod
without imagination, circling
the same sombre garden
with its fountain dry in the forecourt,
the gri-gri palms desiccating
dung pods like goats,
the same lines rule the White Papers,
the same steps ascend Whitehall,
and only the name of the fool changes
under the plumed white cork-hat
for the Independence Parades,
revolving around, in calypso,
to the brazen joy of the tubas.

Why are the eyes of the beautiful
and unmarked children
in the uniforms of the country
bewildered and shy,
why do they widen in terror
of the pride drummed into their minds?
Were they truer, the old songs,
when the law lived far away,
when the veiled queen, her girth
as comfortable as cushions,
upheld the orb with its stern admonitions?

72

We wait for the changing of statues,
for the change of parades.

Here he comes now, here he comes!
Papa! Papa! With his crowd,
the sleek, waddling seals of his Cabinet,
trundling up to the dais,
as the wind puts its tail between
the cleft of the mountain, and a wave
coughs once, abruptly.
Who will name this silence
respect? Those forced, hoarse hosannas
awe? That tin-ringing tune
from the pumping, circling horns
the New World? Find a name
for that look on the faces
of the electorate. Tell me
how it all happened, and why
I said nothing.

The Wind in the Dooryard

(for Eric Roach)

I didn't want this poem to come
from the torn mouth,
I didn't want this poem to come
from his salt body,

but I will tell you what he celebrated:

He writes of the wall with spilling coralita
from the rim of the rich garden,

and the clean dirt yard
clean as the parlour table
with a yellow tree
an ackee, an almond
a pomegranate
in the clear vase of sunlight,

sometimes he put his finger
on the pulse of the wind,
when he heard the sea in the cedars.
He went swimming to Africa,
but he felt tired;
he chose that way
to reach his ancestors.

No, I did not want to write this,
but, doesn't the sunrise
force itself through the curtain
of the trembling eyelids?
When the cows are statues in the misting field
that sweats out the dew,
and the horse lifts its iron head
and the jaws of the sugar mules
ruminate and grind like the factory?

I did not want to hear it again,
the echo of broken windmills,
the mutter of the wild yams creeping
over the broken palings,
the noise of the moss
stitching the stone barracoons,

but the rain breaks
on the foreheads of the wild yams,
the dooryard opens the voice
of his rusty theme,

and the first quick drops of the drizzle
the libations to Shango
dry fast as sweat on the forehead
and our tears also.

The peasant reeks sweetly of bush,
he smells the same as his donkey –
they smell of the high, high country
of clouds and stunted pine –
the man wipes his hand
that is large as a yam
and as crusty with dirt
across the tobacco-stained
paling stumps of his torn mouth,
he rinses with the mountain dew,
and he spits out pity.

I did not want it to come,
but sometimes, under the armpit
of the hot sky over the country
the wind smells of salt
and a certain breeze lifts
the sprigs of the coralita
as if, like us,
lifting our heads, at our happiest,
it too smells the freshness of life.

The Bright Field

My nerves steeled against the power of London,
  hurried home that evening, with the sense
we all have, of the crowd's hypocrisy,

to feel my rage, turned on in self-defence,
bear mercy for the anonymity
of every self humbled by massive places,
and I, who moved against a bitter sea,
was moved by the light on Underground-bound faces.

Their sun that would not set was going down
on their flushed faces, brickwork like a kiln,
on pillar-box-bright buses between trees,
with the compassion of calendar art;
like walking sheaves of harvest, the quick crowd
thickened in separate blades of cane or wheat
from factories and office doors conveyed
to one end by the loud belt of the street.
And that end brings its sadness, going in
by Underground, by cab, by bullock-cart,
and lances us with punctual, maudlin
pity down lanes or cane-fields, till the heart,
seeing, like dark canes, the river-spires sharpen,
feels an involuntary bell begin
to toll for everything, even in London,
heart of our history, original sin.

The vision that brought Samuel Palmer peace,
that stoked Blake's fury at her furnaces,
flashes from doormen's buttons and the rocks
around Balandra. These slow belfry-strokes –
cast in the pool of London, from which swallows
rise in wide rings, and from their bright field, rooks –
mark the same beat by which a pelican goes
across Salybia as the tide lowers.

Dark August

So much rain, so much life like the swollen sky
of this black August. My sister, the sun,
broods in her yellow room and won't come out.

Everything goes to hell; the mountains fume
like a kettle, rivers overrun; still,
she will not rise and turn off the rain.

She's in her room, fondling old things,
my poems, turning her album. Even if thunder falls
like a crash of plates from the sky,

she does not come out.
Don't you know I love you but am hopeless
at fixing the rain? But I am learning slowly

to love the dark days, the steaming hills,
the air with gossiping mosquitoes,
and to sip the medicine of bitterness,

so that when you emerge, my sister,
parting the beads of the rain,
with your forehead of flowers and eyes of forgiveness,

all will not be as it was, but it will be true
(you see they will not let me love
as I want), because, my sister, then

I would have learnt to love black days like bright ones,
the black rain, the white hills, when once
I loved only my happiness and you.

Sea Canes

Half my friends are dead.
I will make you new ones, said earth.
No, give me them back, as they were, instead,
with faults and all, I cried.

Tonight I can snatch their talk
from the faint surf's drone
through the canes, but I cannot walk

on the moonlit leaves of ocean
down that white road alone,
or float with the dreaming motion

of owls leaving earth's load.
O earth, the number of friends you keep
exceeds those left to be loved.

The sea-canes by the cliff flash green and silver
they were the seraph lances of my faith,
but out of what is lost grows something stronger

that has the rational radiance of stone,
enduring moonlight, further than despair,
strong as the wind, that through dividing canes

brings those we love before us, as they were,
with faults and all, not nobler, just there.

Oddjob, a Bull Terrier

You prepare for one sorrow,
but another comes.
It is not like the weather,
you cannot brace yourself,
the unreadiness is all.
Your companion, the woman,
the friend next to you,
the child at your side,
and the dog,
we tremble for them,
we look seaward and muse
it will rain.
We shall get ready for rain;
you do not connect
the sunlight altering
the darkening oleanders
in the sea-garden,
the gold going out of the palms.
You do not connect this,
the fleck of the drizzle
on your flesh
with the dog's whimper,
the thunder doesn't frighten,
the readiness is all;
what follows at your feet
is trying to tell you
the silence is all:
it is deeper than the readiness,
it is sea-deep,
earth-deep,
love-deep.

The silence
is stronger than thunder,
we are stricken dumb and deep
as the animals who never utter love
as we do, except
it becomes unutterable
and must be said,
in a whimper,
in tears,
in the drizzle that comes to our eyes
not uttering the loved thing's name,
the silence of the dead,
the silence of the deepest buried love is
the one silence,
and whether we bear it for beast,
for child, for woman, or friend,
it is the one love, it is the same,
and it is blest
deepest by loss
it is blest, it is blest.

Earth

Let the day grow on you upward
through your feet,
the vegetal knuckles,

to your knees of stone,
until by evening you are a black tree;
feel, with evening,

the swifts thicken your hair,
the new moon rising out of your forehead,
and the moonlit veins of silver

running from your armpits
like rivulets under white leaves.
Sleep, as ants

cross over your eyelids.
You have never possessed anything
as deeply as this.

This is all you have owned
from the first outcry
through forever;

you can never be dispossessed.

To Return to the Trees

(for John Figueroa)

Senex, an oak.
Senex, this old sea-almond
unwincing in spray

in this geriatric grove
on the sea-road to Cumana.
To return to the trees,

to decline like this tree,
the burly oak
of Boanerges Ben Jonson!

Or, am I lying
like this felled almond
when I write I look forward to age –

a gnarled poet
bearded with the whirlwind,
his metres like thunder?

It is not only the sea,
no, for on windy, green mornings
I read the changes on Morne Coco Mountain,

from flagrant sunrise
to its ashen end;
grey has grown strong to me,

it's no longer neutral,
no longer the dirty flag
of courage going under,

it is speckled with hues
like quartz, it's as
various as boredom,

grey now is a crystal
haze, a dull diamond,
stone-dusted and stoic,

grey is the heart at peace,
tougher than the warrior
as it bestrides factions,

it is the great pause
when the pillars of the temple
rest on Samson's palms

and are held, held,
that moment
when the heavy rock of the world

like a child sleeps
on the trembling shoulders of Atlas
and his own eyes close,

the toil that is balance.
Seneca, that fabled bore,
and his gnarled, laborious Latin

I can read only in fragments
of broken bark, his
heroes tempered by whirlwinds,

who see with the word
senex, with its two eyes,
through the boles of this tree,

beyond joy,
beyond lyrical utterance,
this obdurate almond

going under the sand
with this language, slowly,
by sand grains, by centuries.

Selections from

The Star-Apple Kingdom

Sabbaths, WI

Those villages stricken with the melancholia of Sunday,
in all of whose ochre streets one dog is sleeping

those volcanoes like ashen roses, or the incurable sore
of poverty, around whose puckered mouth thin boys are
selling yellow sulphur stone

the burnt banana leaves that used to dance
the river whose bed is made of broken bottles
the cocoa grove where a bird whose cry sounds green and
yellow and in the lights under the leaves crested with
orange flame has forgotten its flute

gommiers peeling from sunburn still wrestling to escape the
  sea

the dead lizard turning blue as stone

those rivers, threads of spittle, that forgot the old music

that dry, brief esplanade under the drier sea almonds
where the dry old men sat

watching a white schooner stuck in the branches
and playing draughts with the moving frigate birds

those hillsides like broken pots
those ferns that stamped their skeletons on the skin

and those roads that begin reciting their names at vespers

86

mention them and they will stop
those crabs that were willing to let an epoch pass
those herons like spinsters that doubted their reflections
inquiring, inquiring

those nettles that waited
those Sundays, those Sundays

those Sundays when the lights at the road's end were an
    occasion

those Sundays when my mother lay on her back
those Sundays when the sisters gathered like white moths
round their street lantern

and cities passed us by on the horizon

Forest of Europe

(for Joseph Brodsky)

The last leaves fell like notes from a piano
and left their ovals echoing in the ear;
with gawky music stands, the winter forest
looks like an empty orchestra, its lines
ruled on these scattered manuscripts of snow.

The inlaid copper laurel of an oak
shines through the brown-bricked glass above your head
as bright as whisky, while the wintry breath
of lines from Mandelstam, which you recite,
uncoils as visibly as cigarette smoke.

'The rustling of rouble notes by the lemon Neva.'
Under your exile's tongue, crisp under heel,
the gutturals crackle like decaying leaves,
the phrase from Mandelstam circles with light
in a brown room, in barren Oklahoma.

There is a Gulag Archipelago
under this ice, where the salt, mineral spring
of the long Trail of Tears runnels these plains
as hard and open as a herdsman's face
sun-cracked and stubbled with unshaven snow.

Growing in whispers from the Writers' Congress,
the snow circles like cossacks round the corpse
of a tired Choctaw till it is a blizzard
of treaties and white papers as we lose
sight of the single human through the cause.

So every spring these branches load their shelves,
like libraries with newly published leaves,
till waste recycles them – paper to snow –
but, at zero of suffering, one mind
lasts like this oak with a few brazen leaves.

As the train passed the forest's tortured icons,
the floes clanging like freight yards, then the spires
of frozen tears, the stations screeching steam,
he drew them in a single winter's breath
whose freezing consonants turned into stones.

He saw the poetry in forlorn stations
under clouds vast as Asia, through districts
that could gulp Oklahoma like a grape,
not these tree-shaded prairie halts but space
so desolate it mocked destinations.

Who is that dark child on the parapets
of Europe, watching the evening river mint
its sovereigns stamped with power, not with poets,
the Thames and the Neva rustling like banknotes,
then, black on gold, the Hudson's silhouettes?

From frozen Neva to the Hudson pours,
under the airport domes, the echoing stations,
the tributary of emigrants whom exile
has made as classless as the common cold,
citizens of a language that is now yours,

and every February, every 'last autumn',
you write far from the threshing harvesters
folding wheat like a girl plaiting her hair,
far from Russia's canals quivered with sunstroke,
a man living with English in one room.

The tourist archipelagos of my South
are prisons too, corruptible, and though
there is no harder prison than writing verse,
what's poetry, if it is worth its salt,
but a phrase men can pass from hand to mouth?

From hand to mouth, across the centuries,
the bread that lasts when systems have decayed,
when, in his forest of barbed-wire branches,
a prisoner circles, chewing the one phrase
whose music will last longer than the leaves,

whose condensation is the marble sweat
of angels' foreheads, which will never dry
till Borealis shuts the peacock lights
of its slow fan from L.A. to Archangel,
and memory needs nothing to repeat.

Frightened and starved, with divine fever
Osip Mandelstam shook, and every
metaphor shuddered him with ague,
each vowel heavier than a boundary stone,
'to the rustling of rouble notes by the lemon Neva',

but now that fever is a fire whose glow
warms our hands, Joseph, as we grunt like primates
exchanging gutturals in this winter cave
of a brown cottage, while in drifts outside
mastodons force their systems through the snow.

The Schooner Flight

Chapter 11: After the Storm

There's a fresh light that follows a storm
while the whole sea still havoc; in its bright wake
I saw the veiled face of Maria Concepcion
marrying the ocean, then drifting away
in the widening lace of her bridal train
with white gulls her bridesmaids, till she was gone.
I wanted nothing after that day.
Across my own face, like the face of the sun,
a light rain was falling, with the sea calm.

Fall gently, rain, on the sea's upturned face
like a girl showering; make these islands fresh
as Shabine once knew them! Let every trace,
every hot road, smell like clothes she just press
and sprinkle with drizzle. I finish dream;
whatever the rain wash and the sun iron:
the white clouds, the sea and sky with one seam,

is clothes enough for my nakedness.
Though my *Flight* never pass the incoming tide
of this inland sea beyond the loud reefs
of the final Bahamas, I am satisfied
if my hand gave voice to one people's grief.
Open the map. More islands there, man,
than peas on a tin plate, all different size, '
one thousand in the Bahamas alone,
from mountains to low scrub with coral keys,
and from this bowsprit, I bless every town,
the blue smell of smoke in hills behind them,
and the one small road winding down them like twine
to the roofs below; I have only one theme:

The bowsprit, the arrow, the longing, the lunging heart—
the flight to a target whose aim we'll never know,
vain search for one island that heals with its harbour
and a guiltless horizon, where the almond's shadow
doesn't injure the sand. There are so many islands!
As many islands as the stars at night
on that branched tree from which meteors are shaken
like falling fruit around the schooner *Flight*.
But things must fall, and so it always was,
on the one hand Venus, on the other Mars;
all, and are one, just as this earth is one
island in archipelagos of stars.
My first friend was the sea. Now, is my last.
I stop talking now. I work, then I read,
catching under a lantern hooked to the mast.
I try to forget what happiness was,
and when that don't work, I study the stars.
Sometimes is just me, and the soft-scissored foam
as the deck turn white and the moon open
a cloud like a door, and the light over me
is a road in white moonlight taking me home.
Shabine sang to you from the depths of the sea.

Notes to the Poems

Notes to the Poems

The Harbour

A young poet's meditation on his choice of sacred over profane love, 'The Harbour' contrasts the lonely, imperilled journeying of a soul seeking illumination through art with the 'safe twilight' available to one content with human love – though that love obfuscates vision ('raises walls') and is subject moreover to Time. The poem proceeds via ironic parallels. The 'old lies' of the lover are 'bitter and sly' but the poet too is engaged in 'an antique hoax' (since illumination is ultimately inaccessible?) and therefore drowning, though a different drowning, awaits each, the lover sinking into bemusement ('since feelings drown'), the poet (l. 14) into madness, perhaps; and while the poem plainly proffers a view of the poet's heroism, the lover also has his 'secret faring-forth'. None of this quite saves the young Walcott from self-dramatization, or from a certain smugness in that dismissal of 'the secure from thinking' – but the tone of the poem is melancholy rather than assertive, and its last, withdrawing image gives a scale: in comparison with the immensity of Life the poet is himself a mere paddler.

The theme of 'The Harbour' is archetypal (read, for instance, the short chapter, 'The Lee Shore', from Melville's *Moby Dick*) and the religious significance, for the poet, of the initial image is elsewhere made explicit, in the line (from 'Sainte Lucie', published a quarter of a century later) 'your faith like a canoe at evening coming in'. But its chief delights lie elsewhere: in the voluptuous sibilance (characteristic of serpents and seas) which pervades the whole poem; in the dynamism of the fifth line, its lurch, pause, surge and collapse mimetic of a wave of the sea; in the languor of all those long vowels. Notice also how nearly physical is that difficult spondee 'humped hills' (in its context, a sexual image); how the sunny certainties of the traditional sonnet's rhyme scheme are first darkened by half-rhymes (dusk/ask, move/gave) and then abandoned altogether; how the preponderance of heavy stresses in the last line brings the poem to its 'dying fall' – and how, amid the calm vowels of that line, the diphthong denotes the horror.

To a Painter in England

The poem begins by contrasting 'cities of fog' with 'personal islands' (consider the aptness of the rhyme: industry/I). In the succeeding verses, however, the poet's attitudes to the English city and the Caribbean are abruptly reversed – so much so that 'sicken' (l. 4), for which 'yearn' might have appeared a synonym, virtually reverts, after the nervous exhaustion of v. 3, to its literal meaning. With v. 4 it becomes apparent that what has prompted this turnabout – as it stands, a confusion in the poem – is the writer's sense of his own inadequacy as a painter (which the young Walcott had hoped to be). Thus the island is 'virginal', the trees 'spinsterish', because they remain 'unpossessed' by the artist. None the less, the poet affirms, there survives in him an impulse to bless – a specifically religious impulse, though Walcott is at pains to dissociate it from the 'Sabbath logic' of Christianity and to assert the 'decision' of the individual soul. 'Silence' (v. 5, l. 6) in that state of grace is brimful: the womb of speech (cf. 'And the Word was made flesh, and the Word *was* flesh').

An enduring strength of Walcott's poetry has been its author's mastery of the iambic pentameter. Notice with what apparent effortlessness the elegant, mannered speech of the first four verses accommodates itself to that line. How does Walcott achieve, in the last verse, the change of tone which lifts it to declamation and dénouement?

Gauguins (v. 1, l. 4): Paul Gauguin, French post-impressionist painter (1848–1903), who, seduced by their beauty and the apparent wholeness of their (pre-industrial) cultures, lived and painted in both Martinique and Tahiti.

Discloses around corners an architecture (v. 5, l. 2): The image is of turning a corner and coming into sight of a church.

Ruins of a Great House

Descriptive, narrative and meditative by turn, 'Ruins of a Great House' conveys the experience of having one's conventional responses to the iniquities of West Indian history subverted: first, by perplexity at the evident coexistence of beauty and evil – yoked so in the phrase 'murderers and poets' – and secondly, by a sense of the impermanence of all human achievement. Images of death predominate: limes, ash. Empires rise only to fall, and in the end it is always the crow, the worm and the mouse which are the victors. It occurs to Walcott that the gulf between slaveowner and slave is not so great as to obscure their essential brotherhood and common destiny in time – the grave. Time, furthermore, may heal – 'The river flows, obliterating hurt' – and thus the attempt at rage rings false; consider that voluptuous 'manorial' in the penultimate verse. In the last verse the poem reclaims a response appropriate to its central lament: 'Deciduous beauty prospered and is gone'.

disjecta membra (v. 1, l. 1): Scattered components. From Horace's 'disjecti membra poetae'.

Great House (v. 1, l. 1): The principal and most ostentatious dwelling-place on a plantation, usually occupied by the owner or manager.

Marble as Greece (v. 4, l. 1): Marble is limestone in a crystalline state. It was extensively used by the Greeks in architecture and sculpture in the time of the Grecian Empire.

Faulkner's (v. 4, l. 1): William Faulkner (1897–1962). American novelist and recipient of the Nobel Prize for Literature (1949), Faulkner saw the American South as condemned by its sinful exploitation of land and man. In his novels he explored the phenomenon of personal and social disintegration, charted the persistence of the past into the present, and affirmed the virtue of endurance.

Kipling (v. 6, l. 6): Rudyard Kipling (1865–1936). English writer famous for his poems and stories set in India – the country of his birth and at that time part of the British Empire.

Hawkins, Walter Raleigh, Drake (v. 7, l. 3): English adventurers and pirates who operated in the West Indies and the Spanish Main during and just after the reign of Elizabeth I, when England was the dominant maritime power in Europe. Raleigh was also a poet.

The rot remains with us, the men are gone (v. 7, l. 8): Cf. Shakespeare *Julius Caesar*: 'The evil that men do lives after them.'

Donne (v. 7, l. 11): John Donne (1572–1631). English metaphysic poet and author of the famous passage beginning: 'No man is an island, entire of itself; every man is a part of the continent, a part of the main. If a clod be washed away, Europe is the less, as well as if manor of thy friend's or thine own were . . .'

Albion (v. 8, l. 4): Old poetic name for Britain, perhaps derived from its white (Latin: *albus*) cliffs visible from the coast of Gaul (France).

Tales of the Islands: Chapter III
One of a sequence of sonnets in which Walcott departs from the conventional form by largely eschewing rhyme. Chapter III nonetheless falls naturally into the Petrarchan sonnet's division into octet and sestet. The theme ('la belle qui fut') is similar to that of 'Ruins...' ('Deciduous beauty prospered and is gone') but its treatment here is both funnier and more horrific. The poem should be read in a tone of exaggerated wonder, a burlesque of wonder – the tone of a parent reading a bedtime story to a small enthralled child. The technique is ironic; the effect depends on the dissociation between what is being said and how it is being said.

lazaretto (l. 1): A hospital for the diseased poor, especially lepers.

Magdalen of Donatello (l. 5): Donatello (diminutive of Donato) was a Florentine sculptor (1386–1466), one of the founders of Renaissance art. The 'Magdalen' belongs to his final creative phase, which was marked by a new depth of psychological insight, and in which the powerful torsos found in his earlier work became withered and spidery – overwhelmed, as it were, by tremendous emotional tensions.

Tales of the Islands: Chapter X
The last of the sonnet sequence, it is also the one in which rhyme reappears. (To what effect, do you think?) The scenario is one of departure; the repeated 'I watched' evokes the young man's nostalgia for his receding island, as do the lovingly observed details (with perhaps one lapse: difficult to see the fuselage from inside the plane). The poem is placed in its autobiographical context in Chapter 17 of Walcott's later book, *Another Life*. Account, if you can, for the peculiar, cathartic power of the last line.

A Careful Passion
'A Careful Passion' (and as the poem unfolds the title is seen to be self-accusing rather than paradoxical) evokes the sensations of a man engaged in quitting an adulterous affair – like that 'old Greek freighter quitting port'. Bored and disaffected, he allows his mind to wander back to another past love (v. 2, ll. 3–5) and is in consequence disturbed by a sense of life as meaninglessly repetitive: a succession of waves on

sand, or an old windmill vacantly turning – the latter the hidden image underlying 'the rusty cries/Of gulls revolving in the wind'. His attempt at stoicism (v. 3, l. 4) fails – the line discloses instead sententiousness and self-pity – and, failing, releases an image of death, in particular of spiritual death: 'eyes full of sand'. Dissociation (v. 3, l. 8) and self-mockery follow.

'A Careful Passion' is less about the death of love than about an inability to love. It is about the way in which 'the self-seeking heart . . . desperate for some mirror', engenders its own alienation, forcing its owner into the role of actor, and thus of cynic. Though the theme is hardly original, the experience comes over as felt, and the poem's near-perfect marriage of subject matter and form makes it almost entirely successful. Consider, for example, how the predominance of end-stopped lines, each reinforced by rhyme, enacts the narrator's ennui and isolation; or how several apparently artless descriptive details (those tables 'fixed like islands', that 'freighter quitting port', those 'coupling flies', the wind playing 'with the corners of her skirt', the street 'brightening', but with sunset, vanguard of night) contribute to the thematic unity of the poem; or the appropriateness of the feminine rhyme with which the poem closes. Notice also how the 'city's edge . . . harbour's edge' are resolved into the thrice-repeated 'water's edge'. (Water: traditionally a symbol of passion, but also the mirror which enticed the 'self-seeking' Narcissus to his death.)

(An amusing insight into the exigencies of metre is provided by that ungrammatical comma near the end of v. 2, l. 6. The lines 'The hand which wears her husband's ring lies on/The table idly, a brown leaf on the sand' are pentameters, and almost certainly existed in this form in an earlier draft of the poem. The poet, however, for the sake of the pun, decided to stop the first line at 'lies' – and then found himself with a problem of scansion. This he 'solved' by inserting the comma, the pause it denotes standing for the initial unstressed syllable of the last foot of that line.)

Castiliane

In 'Castiliane' Walcott attempts to enrich his actual environment – perceived as vaguely sordid, with its heat, flies, and 'odours of the port' – by invoking into it the fabled centuries of Spain, or of Spanish culture as manifested in the Caribbean. As the incarnation of that culture the poet imagines 'a wraith . . . frail Donna'. The vision i tenuous; reality (section II, v. 2) keeps breaking in, and even when it doesn't the poet is forced wryly to admit that his wraith would probably have ended up married to some 'goldtoothed' merchant, 'a man who hawks and profits in this heat', since 'whoever lived by verse?' 'Castiliane' is escapism consciously indulged in; yet in the final verse (in which the tone of the poem grows serious) the poet affirms the endurance of the wraith as the 'ancient, simple spirit' of a traditional – if now debased – culture.

A lighter look at love than 'A Careful Passion' affords, 'Castiliane' strikes a note of idle fancy uncharacteristic of Walcott's poetry (though frequently in evidence in his plays). There is a sense of the poet at his ease, allowing imagination the range of its whimsy, and indulging in the music of words – the latter to effects at times both gorgeous and funny, as in the first five lines of the last verse of section II. The product of this playfulness is none the less impressive; the poem seems effortlessly accomplished.

Golondrina (v. 1, l. 1): Spanish for 'swallow' (the bird).

noon's despair (v. 1, l. 10): T. S. Eliot quotes Emerson as saying that 'the lengthened shadow of a man is history'. Noon, the shadowless time, may represent the poet's sense of the absence of history, of connection.

fin de siècle (v. 3, l. 4): Invoking characteristics of the late nineteenth century, the phrase has connotations of decadence.

Alhambras (v. 3, l. 6): The Alhambra was the fortress of the Moorish monarchs of Granada, built in the Middle Ages.

da Falla (v. 5, l. 2): Manuel de Falla (1876–1946), a Spanish nationalist composer, born in Cadiz, whose compositions include music for the bullring.

A Lesson for this Sunday

In another poem Walcott writes of travelling by train through an idyllic landscape, then concludes sadly: 'Why feel that had we found them earlier some good/Could come out of a country change? We would/have spoiled such places too . . .' The theme of 'A Lesson for this Sunday' is, likewise, man's irruption into Paradise. Since the butterfly's tormentors are small children, the liberal argument – that it is our upbringing which warps us away from a predisposition to good – cannot hold; the poet is forced to recognize 'Heredity of cruelty everywhere', and thus to reconsider the meaning of free will.

Because it does not go beyond stating that dismaying realization, 'A Lesson for this Sunday' remains a minor poem. None the less it exhibits the density and unity of a little masterpiece. Consider the relationships between 'simple praise' and 'mantis prays'; between 'lemon frock' and 'the frocks of summer'; between 'my hammock swings' and 'the mind swings'; between 'Crouched on plump haunches' and 'shrieks to eviscerate its abdomen'. Notice how in the first verse the absence of punctuation and the sibilant, regular lines suggest a dreaming, undisturbed world – until, with its abrupt parenthesis (v. 2, l. 1) the human voice arrives.

The last line both echoes and modifies the first: to what effect? How would the poem have differed if the poet had carried the ironic approach (begun at v. 2, l. 4 and abandoned seven lines later) through to the conclusion of the poem? At several places in the poem Walcott suggests an identification between the girl and the butterfly; can you identify these? How does this identification modify the meaning of the poem? What is implied by reference to the scythe's 'design'?

Allegre

One of the few free verse poems in In a Green Night, 'Allegre' seems written rather for the West Indian conversational voice, which favours the anapaest, than for the slowed and heightened speech characteristic of the iambic pentameter. The effect of spontaneity is reinforced by the 'artless' piling on of details – 'And the sunward sides . . . And the slopes' – and is as appropriate here, given the poem's theme, as it would have been incongruous in, say, a ruminative poem like 'Ruins of a Great House'.

Elsewhere Walcott has written: 'I may have many sorrows,/Dawn is not one of them'. 'Allegre' is for the most part a celebration of dawn, of youth. The day, the poet and the country are young and the morning is 'full of elation'. But Walcott is essentially a meditative poet, so it is not surprising that towards the end of the poem the mood changes. (Consider also the remark of the American poet Robert Frost, that a poem 'should begin in delight and end in wisdom'.) Two of the three lines beginning with 'No temples . . .' state what seem to

Walcott to be paradoxes (which are they?) and the poet is moved to caution: as the sky is loveliest when the earth is barren, so the elation may be 'useless and empty' so long as the 'true self' remains undiscovered.

The last eight lines of 'Allegre' seem to invite discussions of an historical and philosophical nature. Are West Indians rootless? In what sense can elation be 'useless' – or, for that matter, useful? It may be a flaw of the poem that the assertions these lines contain are contradicted by an earlier image, 'The roots of delight growing downward', which suggests that it is possible to *put down* roots (as well as to emerge from them) and that delight (elation) can achieve this. It may also be mentioned that an older Walcott in several of his later poems implicitly disavows the doubts at the end of 'Allegre' – consider, for example, 'Names' (for Edward Brathwaite), or the fact that in 'Commune' it is the snake which hisses 'this is not enough,/ neither the love nor the work of love enough'.

The roots of delight growing downward, /As the singer in his prime (v. 3, ll. 2–3): An image, presumably, of the way that a baritone at the crescendo of his song seems increasingly 'rooted' at his hands, palm upward, rise. Cf. Ezra Pound: 'What thou lovest well is thy true country'.

The stream keeps its edges, wind-honed (v. 5, l. 1): Obscure, since it is difficult to imagine the wind 'honing' either a stream or its edges. The remainder of the verse claims the detachment of the intellect from the affective life, and thus prepares us for the intrusion of intellectual concerns upon the pastoral scene.

Conqueror

The obdurate consonants of the opening line aptly introduce the conqueror: an 'Iron deliverer' (a comprehensive pun) with 'the wet-metal blaze/Of the sun in his sunken eye'. (Why 'sunken', do you think?) We are not prepared for his appearance; like a creation of the 'still, directionless hour' itself he is suddenly there, immobile.

We are familiar with this figure. His latter-day counterpart is the lone cowboy silhouetted on the ridge at dusk, overlooking the unsuspecting town. Both are 'men of iron', transformed by some purpose which overrides the natural man, and it is this aspect of the conqueror, the violence which the god or purpose in him enacts against his 'human' nature, which engages Walcott's imagination. In v. 2 he states the conqueror's predicament; in v. 3, with the description of the ongoing rural life of the valley, he further implies it – from that idyll the man of iron is excluded. Furthermore, his conquests must necessarily be incomplete (consider the function in the poem of 'those unconquered peaks').

Yet for all that, the conqueror is the embodiment of one of 'nature's laws', which the rhyme identifies. (Look again at 'A Lesson for this Sunday'.) In a diversion constituted by the last eight lines of v. 3, Walcott, as in 'A Lesson' and 'Allegre', questions the validity of the pastoral dream, 'the quiet of unknowing'. The 'small, furred beast' (which reappears many years later – see 'Mass Man') frighteningly dramatizes the conqueror's work; the sparrows, 'Fables of innocence . . . Or natural thoughts', are poignantly contrasted with 'that armed mass quiet on [the hidden side of] the hill'.

Where in the poem, and why, is the conqueror referred to as 'it'? How effective is the description of the soldiers' lances as 'iron sheaves'? Why should 'joy remembered make rage the more'? And, assuming that the rhythm of the poem's last five lines constitute an attempt to mime the actions they describe or imply (including the conqueror's horse moving joltingly off downhill) how would you react to the suggestion that the penultimate line should be made into a regular pentameter by removing the word 'sighing'?

'Conqueror' describes an imaginary painting. Does this information help you to understand or appreciate the poem? In what way(s)?

The Castaway

In another Walcott poem, 'Crusoe's Island', the 'bearded hermit' succeeds in stocking his 'Eden' with 'all the joys/But one/Which sent him howling for a human voice'. 'The Castaway', likewise, delineates an experience of isolation. The castaway's hunger for human company ('a sail') brings him close to hysteria – to a state in which any action would quickly become frenzied. Even lying still he hallucinates, perceiving himself as 'sailing' – i.e. piloting – the 'ribbed shadow' of a palm frond stirring above him (an echo perhaps of Coleridge's 'The Ancient Mariner', in which a vessel approaching the doomed ship of the mariner turns out to be a 'spectre-ship' with

'naked ribs' through which the low sun peers. A comparable halluci-
nation afflicts the sailor-narrator of Walcott's 'The Schooner *Flight*').

Verses 4–7 evoke the natural world, engaged in its unhurried,
aimless, eternal routines. In this world, only the castaway is capable
of giving a scale; and when, 'cracking a sea-louse', he declares that he
has made 'thunder split' (and is thus 'Godlike') the reader is prepared
for the gesture of despair with which the poem closes, the renuncia-
tion of both selfhood and the world.

You should recognize, however, that Walcott is not the castaway
but the castaway's creator – and thus capable of commenting
(implicitly) on the behaviour of his creature. With this in mind, look
again at the last three verses. Notice that while the catalogue of 'dead
metaphors' is ostensibly there to tell us what the castaway is renounc-
ing, our final experience of the poem is not of his renunciation but of
the metaphors themselves. Is it possible, do you think, that while
establishing the fact of the castaway's despair Walcott means us to
take a very different impression from these lines? What do you make
of that oblique reference to the crucifixion of Christ (the Redeemer)
with which the poem ends?

In formal terms, a defining characteristic of *The Castaway* (the collec-
tion which takes its title from the present poem) is Walcott's struggle
against his own predisposition towards the iambic pentameter – a
struggle evident in the fact that many lines which were obviously
composed as pentameters to begin with, are broken up or run on in
the final version (e.g. 'Blowing sand, thin as smoke,/Bored, shifts its
dunes', or 'the rage with which the sandfly's head is filled'). And to
students coming to 'The Castaway' from the poems of *In a Green Night*
it may also be evident that the texture of the poems has changed. (Can
you say in what ways?) Do you see any connection between the two
developments – the formal and the textural? (What would you make
of the charge that 'The Castaway', while more immediately effective
than, say, 'The Harbour', is also less 'resonant'?)

The Swamp
Here are three interpretations of 'The Swamp':

(1) The historical: The consciousness behind 'The Swamp' is that of a
white American from the Deep South of slavery ('cracker convicts,
Negroes'). He senses that the 'black mouth[s]' threaten the

civilization ('highway') he has erected among them; that his culture is progressively enervated by their 'black mood'; and that somewhere along 'the road ahead' – i.e. in the future – he will lose his racial memory ('go black with widening amnesia'), whereupon their 'chaos' will overrun everything. The poem thus presents that familiar historical phenomenon, the colonizer's fear and loathing, born of guilt, of those whom he has colonized.

(2) The psychological: 'The Swamp' presents in metaphorical terms a struggle between the ego and the id, and premonishes the eventual triumph of the latter. In it, as in one of Tennessee Williams's fantastical gardens, the denizens of the unconscious press forward, suffocating the ego ('highway') – that is, the individual's sense of selfhood – with images of an infernal and promiscuous paradise (vv. 6–7). Even while the ego protests (v. 8), it is drowning in the 'fast-filling night'. Soon, the last bird 'drinks darkness', amnesia encroaches upon the ego, and in the orgiastic image with which the final verse opens we perceive the triumph of the id: the confusion of different parts of the body into a 'knot' implying the breakdown of self-awareness, and thus the advent of 'chaos'.

(3) The philosophical: The affirmation latent in 'The Swamp' is that there exists an indissoluble relationship between order and life: death, it is argued, may be less cessation than a kind of biological insanity – a return to the primordial 'knot'. In equating a swamp's teeming confusion with 'limbo' and the void (by which 'nothing', v. 4, l. 1, is translatable) the poet implies the primacy of the quiddity of things, thus adding a spiritual dimension to life.

Which interpretation do you prefer? (Why?) Is it possible that all three are valid? If so, what does this tell you about (1) the nature of poetry; (2) the pitfalls of criticism? Notice, however, that we cannot adequately describe the achievement or effect of the poem without also considering its language – e.g. the part played by those horrific aspirates (ll. 2 and 8) and dark vowels (in: home, growth, hero, shallows, mangrove, toad, road, throat) in *creating* the 'black mood' of 'The Swamp'.

Hemingway's hero (v. 3, l. 3): From Ernest Hemingway's story, 'Big Two-Hearted River': 'He did not feel like going on into the swamp . . . In the swamp fishing was a tragic adventure. Nick did not want it.'

The Flock

In 'The Flock' Walcott invokes the virtues of stoicism: austerity, fortitude and constancy ('fixity'). 'The Flock' is a tragic poem, since Walcott realizes (as Shakespeare's Caesar does not) that 'fixity' cannot save a man from 'annihilation' (remember how Shakespeare, with heavy irony, has Caesar killed within twenty lines of proclaiming himself 'constant as the northern star'), and since Walcott also recognizes the existence of a greater 'stoic': Arctic Earth, which – impartial, glacial, and capable of freezing 'giant minds in marble attitudes' – revolves 'with tireless, determined grace/upon an iron axle'. Yet in the final verse the poem achieves a saving balance, an ennobling compromise between the ideal of absolute stoicism – which approaches stoneheartedness – and the enthralled acquiescence of those who, like migratory birds, are prepared to 'blow with the wind'.

'The Flock' opens with an ingenious metaphor out of archery. Notice that the birds – those 'arrows of yearning' – exist at the whim of the seasons. Winter produces their flight, as the mind of the poet produces its own migrating images. (What qualities of the mind do you think the poet means to establish by linking it thus with winter?)

Next, Walcott introduces into that hostile landscape a lone horseman, a 'sepulchral knight'. (Why 'sepulchral'? What similarities do you find between him and the Conqueror of Walcott's earlier poem?) The poet's technique here is cinematic: the knight appears first in close-up ('hooves cannonading snow') and then is rendered from such a distance as to seem 'antlike [on] the forehead of an alp'. (What do you think of the view that, as images of the stature of man, both perspectives may be valid – as in Walcott's witty line, from 'Guyana': 'Ant-sized to God, god to an ant's eyes'?) Is it the horseman or the alp that is crouched 'in iron contradiction' to the weather, or both? Why do you think Walcott renders the alp in anthropomorphic terms?

The knight is both less and more than human: less, in that he is 'Vizor'd with blind defiance' ('Vizor'd': helmeted; but also, in conjunction with 'blind', blinkered); and more, in that his quest is superhuman: what he seeks is nothing less than the source of life itself: a 'yearly divination of the spring'.

In the final lines of the verse Walcott likens the activity of the poet to that of the knight. Both 'travel through ... silence, making dark/

105

symbols . . . across snow [in the poet's case, the white and lifeless page] measuring winter's augury'; and thus, by extension, the poet is also 'sepulchral' (read, in connection with this notion of a poet, W. B. Yeats's 'The Leaders of the Crowd') and his quest is, likewise, to 'claim the centre of life' (Walcott: 'Force').

In the wake of such monumental concerns, and the epic imagery in which they are expressed, the second verse of 'The Flock' comes as a chastening corrective. By comparison with the 'inflexible' grandeur of the world 'as it revolves upon its centuries', man seems transient and inconstant (v. 2, l. 4), prepossessed with images of escape, both his judgements ('condemnation') and his imaginings ('the sun's/exultant larks') ineffectual. The verse thus implies the pathetic diminution of human nature ('antlike' as the knight) when viewed against the backdrop of the cosmos. The question is again one of perspective. Here, as elsewhere, Walcott seems bewitched by the question: since we are human, yet capable at times of seeing through God's eyes, to which perspective should we strive to be true?

The final verse asserts a compromise: a worldview which incorporates elements of both. Thus, while Walcott prays that his mind may reflect the 'fixity' of the world, he rejects its indifference (to the howling of seals and the torn birds), acknowledging instead his human need to 'greet the black wings . . . as a blessing', and for a 'sense of season'. The poem ends in a quietude of acceptance (note that its three feminine line-endings all occur in the last six lines) which tempers, without wholly disowning, the iron argument of its first verse.

'The Flock' is a major poem, and the most accomplished poem in *The Castaway*. It turns upon a balancing of perspectives, and upon wittily established identifications between (1) migratory birds and poetic images; (2) winter and the mind; and (3) knight and poet. Consider the function of metaphor in suggesting these identifications. (In what sense can the 'Arctic' freeze 'minds'?)

Compare the first four lines of 'The Flock' with those of 'The Harbour'. Would you agree with the view that the lines from 'The Flock' seem tauter, yet at the same time more 'arbitrary' than those of the earlier poem? What would you make of the remark that in 'The Flock' Walcott moves away from the poetry of Earth, and into the mansions of the mind?

106

The Whale, His Bulwark

This is a wry poem (but for one flash of anger at those 'derisive, antlike villagers') about the growth of a negative aspect of egalitarianism: the resentful urge to 'humble the high'. Walcott is not interested in anything so banal as 'high society'; his concern, which he later states (in 'Volcano'), is that the capacity for awe, without which people 'are no more than erect ash', has been 'lost to our time': we deride not only grandeur ('majesty') but also the possibility of mystery ('the unfathomable').

In 'The Whale, His Bulwark', as increasingly in his later work, Walcott writes out of the knowledge that in essential concerns he is out of step with his age; and while in some of the later poems his reaction is angry or bitter, in the present poem it is, rather, one of quiet (and embattled: cf. the final line) affirmation. The nostalgia which the poem exhibits in that thrice-repeated 'Once' derives from the poet's memory that not so long ago 'God and a foundered whale were [still] possible' – in the title, 'His' means God's – and his awareness that in the eyes of some readers he will appear to be being perverse is rendered in the ironic repetition of 'yet' (ll. 4 and 18).

Note the aptness of the rhymes to the poem's theme. Verse is cursed; what the Lord raises to our eyes we reduce to pigmy-size; the unfathomable becomes the unfashionable. Consider also the further diminution from the ironic 'mythological' to 'apocryphal' in the light of the references to belief in the first two lines of the last verse. The clause, 'Though the boy may be dead' has at least two meanings; what are they?

Missing the Sea

Imagine living near to a waterfall or wave-breaking beach and waking one morning to discover that its accustomed roar has inexplicably ceased. Your first perception will be of a wrong stillness, a 'deafening absence'; and for some hours perhaps you will have the sensation of walking through 'a thick nothing now' – i.e. a present ('now') which feels oppressively empty, lacking the pressure upon it of the past, and thus any connection to a conceivable future. That sense of being 'estranged' from time – and thus from life – is the state of mind which Walcott evokes in 'Missing the Sea' most tellingly in the image of the

107

newly bereaved unwilling to go on, to accept the onward flow of time, since to do so would be to acquiesce in being carried away (by time) from the beloved, for whom time has stopped.

'Missing the Sea' relies entirely on imagery. Can you think of other images (e.g. the dead hush that comes over trees before rain) that might have found a place in the poem? Without resorting to imagery, attempt to describe the state of mind with which this poem deals. Compare Walcott's poem with what you have written in a brief essay entitled 'The function of imagery'.

The Almond Trees

'The Almond Trees' is an extended metaphor for the enslavement, suffering, endurance, and finally the triumphant 'metamorphosis' into daughters of the grove (i.e. women of the islands) of West Indian women of African descent. In the main successful, it is marred by its one-line verse (heavily redundant, since the identification between woman and tree has already been wittily established by the reference to 'Daphnes', and further realized in vv. 6 and 7) and also – and more damagingly – by the poet in the penultimate verse ascribing to fire a mutilating function, in contradiction to the rest of the poem wherein fire is presented as a curing or refining element: an ambivalence which weakens the triumphant claims of vv. 6 and 7. Notice though how the horrific image of v. 12 (wherein 'holes' means lipless mouths) is defeated in the imagination by the grievous beauty of the last verse.

its spinning rays . . . amaze the sun (v. 3, ll. 3–5): Cf. T. S. Eliot: 'The lengthened shadow of a man/is history, said Emerson'.

the forked limbs of girls toasting their flesh (v. 4, l. 3): The image is of girls sunbathing with legs splayed. It includes connotations of a barbeque – and a satanic pun on 'forked'.

Pompeian bikinis (v. 4, l. 4): In AD 79 several thousand Pompeians living at the foot of Vesuvius perished when that volcano erupted. In many cases the bodies left perfect moulds in the ash. The bikinis may resemble (obscurely?) such moulds. The phrase strengthens the relationship between fire and sexuality latent in the previous line and variously suggested elsewhere in the poem.

brown daphnes (v. 5, l. 1): In classical mythology, Daphne was the daughter of a river-god. Pursued by Apollo, she prayed for help and was turned into a tree.

their furnace (v. 7, l. 5): In the case of the trees, the sun and seablast. In the case of the women, the inferno of forced migration and slavery.

hamadryad's (v. 11, l. 1): In classical mythology, a hamadryad was a nymph living and dying with the tree she inhabited. Walcott may have introduced her (and the pastoral world to which she belonged) in order to destroy, with an emphatic negative ('Not as . . .') the rather too idyllic connotations of the earlier phrase 'brown daphnes'.

Veranda

A poem about the 'unguessed' continuities of life, 'Veranda' falls thematically into three parts. In the first (vv. 1–5) Walcott conjures up the ghosts of representatives of the British Empire – planters, colonels, middlemen and usurers – in the late nineteenth century, when the Empire was 'a fading world' ('flamingo colours': in certain circumstances, e.g. captivity, flamingos fade from their original bright red colour. The quote is from a review by Ronald Bryden of a novel about India). See how many images, all dealing with death, you can unravel and develop from that compressed sentence: 'the sunset furled/round the last post' ('last post' has three meanings).

In the second part (vv. 6–9) the poet recognizes – stepping forth from those 'grey apparitions' – his grandfather's ghost, and the language of the poem changes. Whereas till now it has been dispassionate and ironic ('Planters whose tears were marketable gum', 'usurers whose art/kept an empire in the red'), now, impelled by the poet's memory of his grandfather's migration and death, it moves towards the reverence of cadence ('Sire', and later, 'sir', 'father') and to the consonants of love, those liquid els and esses which lift v. 9 into lyricism. The section ends with the poet's affirmation to his ancestor that 'your genealogical roof tree, fallen, survives . . .' Notice the pathos of the question in v. 8: the ghost cannot speak, the poet must interpret its question, repeat it to be sure.

The final section is dominated by consoling images. Death is but a dream, a sea-crossing, a migration of the soul. The ancestors are sacred (earth, the grave, both enshrines and pardons them), and furthermore the living may redeem the dead. And in a lovely image (v. 11, l. 2) the poet develops the affirmation of continuity made in v. 9. In the light of all this, Walcott asserts his identity with his father and is able to countenance, with calm, the prospect of his own death.

Note that the poet's hand is 'darkening' because (1) he is stepping out of the sun into the shade of the veranda; (2) he is nearing the 'twilight' of the ancestors (i.e. death); and (3) the generations of West Indian Walcotts are each progressively darker-skinned than the last (cf. the reference to his father: 'your mixed son'). Why, and to what effect, does the poem end with a variation (i.e. a varied continuation) of its first line?

In 'Between the Porch and Altar', the American poet Robert Lowell writes: 'The twinkling steel above me is a star;/I am a fallen Christmas tree.' Find in 'Veranda' a pair of lines that echo these, and see if you can demonstrate the similarities in rhythm and cadence between them.

Lampfall

In *Another Life* Walcott writes of being 'balanced at [the] edge by the weight of two dear daughters'. 'Lampfall' likewise re-creates that perilous state of mind in which the impulse to die is held in check – but only just – by love for one's family and friends. Thus the celebration of life encouraged by the 'windy leaves' near the end of v. 1 is at once countered by 'But'; and thenceforth images of alienation predominate. Under the sway of the 'monster' (the deathwish) Walcott perceives himself as being drawn through the inhuman void of deep space, where 'no lights flash ... but the plankton's drifting, phosphorescent stars'. From there he can observe, but can neither be observed (his gaze, 'dead green [and] glaucous', contains no self-reflection) nor be communicated with (his ear is a 'shell'). He feels cut off, far; and in the image of the sea-rock 'Shuttling its white wool' like Penelope, boredom and meaninglessness threaten.

The poem gains in poignancy from certain echoes of Wordsworth's 'Tintern Abbey' (e.g. the lines 'And I'm elsewhere, far as/I shall ever be from you whom I behold now/Dear family, dear friends' recall the earlier poem's 'Oh! yet a little while/May I behold in thee what I was once,/My dear, dear Sister!'). And there are attempts at affirmation: the 'lantern's ring that the sea's/Never extinguished', or the last line

110

of the penultimate verse, wherein Venus is (1) the planet, by which it is possible to navigate; and (2) the goddess of love, the emotion which alone can save us from being lost.

There is, however, an odd change of tone in the final verse. (In fact, it seems less to emerge from the rest of the poem than to undercut it.) Like the desperate, short sentences (and in particular that 'yet') of the penultimate verse, the shift to the past tense is ominous; and in the secondary image of the last line the poem tips towards death. (Note that while the primary image of that line is of technology overrunning everything – beetles=Volkswagens=cars – its secondary meaning is that, as in 'The Swamp' the road ahead threatened to 'merge/Limb, tongue and sinew into a knot', so now the road ahead is increasingly inhabited by beetles. Walcott has also written, in *Another Life*, of 'the path increas[ing] with snakes'.)

the moth-flame metaphor (v. 1, l. 2): Moths are often attracted to (and incinerated by) the heat of lamps, candles, etc. The metaphor is of being drawn to that which kills.

Coleman's (v. 1, l. 3): A Coleman is a lamp whose pressurized fuel emits a steady hum as the mantle burns. The line is probably a metaphor for the human heart poised on the edge of nothingness.

Joseph Wright (v. 1, l. 5): An eighteenth-century American portrait painter who studied in England, his work includes a painting of someone explaining the astrolabe, a graduated circle for taking altitudes at sea. An image of a huddled, lamplit group, the line also prepares us for the later reference to celestial navigation.

Penelope (v. 4, l. 3): In mythology, Penelope, the wife of Odysseus, was often courted by local nobles while her husband was away. She put them off by pretending that she could not remarry until she had finished weaving a shroud for Laertes, Odysseus' father. Every night she unravelled her day's work, so that the shroud was never finished.

This is the fire . . . door of heaven (v. 4, ll. 7–8): Roughly: 'Our dread of losing the warmth of human company prevents us from committing suicide, an act which in Christian religions is punishable by hellfire. Thus to accept human love is to pass through the furnace door into heaven.'

111

Like you (v. 6, l. 1): Presumably a relative or friend; although the person referred to may be Sylvia Plath, an American poet whose posthumously published collection, *Ariel*, was reviewed by Walcott around the same time that 'Lampfall' was written. (Walcott singled out for praise Miss Plath's description of an evening sky 'palely and flamily igniting its carbon monoxide'.) Sylvia Plath committed suicide in 1964. Her poems are generally thought of as bearing witness to the ways in which technology oppresses people.

Ebb

'Ebb' may be read as a poem about alienation and its essential consequence: the erosion of our sense of 'the freshness of life' (Walcott: 'The Wind in the Dooryard') by an unfocused anxiety which sees 'terror in the habitual, miracle . . . in the familiar'. Technology is identified as the enemy of nature (including human nature), and in the first half of the poem Walcott chronicles its assault in these islands. Note the pun on 'fretted'; how an oil slick confounds 'rainbow' with 'muck'; and the connection between 'littered' and 'afterbirth'. The poet is aware that while that 'dark aisle/of fountaining, gold coconuts . . . the last sacred wood' may be an 'oasis' (how rhymed?) or source of spiritual nourishment (cf. 'aisle', 'sacred') it too is marked for demolition. Yet while it survives it contains, 'netted in its weave' (like a ship in a bottle?), the image of an island schooner. An emblem of the spirit of adventure, the 'crippled' survivor of an older, pre-industrial world, the schooner has also been condemned, to irrelevance: 'like the washed-up moon/to circle her lost zone'. (Consider the slang meaning of 'washed-up'.) Walcott disclaims, as inaccessible, the schooner and its world: 'The schooner's out too far,/too far that boyhood'.

Yet in preferring 'safety' to the possibilities of adventure which the schooner represents, Walcott is aware of choosing ignobly: the penultimate verse exhibits a self-accusation sharpened rather than tempered by the claim that 'each sunfall,/the wildest of us all' makes the same choice, and by the guilty belligerence of the ensuing question. The final word of 'Ebb' should therefore be interpreted not as a corroboration of the rest of the verse but rather, in its colloquial sense, as a sardonic expression of disbelief: the disclaimer of a disclaimer. The poem ends in irresolution and self-disgust.

112

In a sense 'Ebb' continues the theme of 'Lampfall'. As an image of meaninglessness, of action which achieves nothing, its 'treadmill' resembles the Penelope of 'Lampfall'; the word 'elsewhere' echoes as sinisterly in the latter poem as in the former; and of course the world of 'Lampfall's last line holds the poet's dismayed attention throughout the first half of 'Ebb'. Where 'Ebb' differs, however, is in the poet's attitude to his choice; the wryness of his observation, in 'Lampfall', of 'the fire that draws us by our dread/Of loss' gives way to the bitter accusation that in choosing 'safety' we 'mortgage life to fear'.

The moon is a traditional symbol of the creative imagination. And elsewhere in the same volume (*The Gulf*) Walcott writes of 'measuring how imagination/ebbs'. Can you substantiate a reading of the poem which suggests it is 'really' about the decline of the creative imagination? How might the advance of industry, which makes obsolete the schooner and her world, endanger the creative imagination itself? What is the function of the punctuation with which the poem ends?

Hawk

In an essay entitled 'On Choosing Port-of-Spain' Walcott writes of Trinidad's Carnival ('a Creole bacchanal') as an 'exultation of the mass will', and describes the Creole mentality as 'the shrillest kind of hedonism, asserting with almost hysterical self-assurance that Trinidad is a paradise', and as 'a particular boastfulness, passing for panache or a sense of the good life . . .'

The boldfaced trochees of 'Hawk' (in Spanish, *gabilan*) mime both the cuatros' 'treng-ka-treng' and the stamping euphoria of Carnival. In all but six lines of the poem Walcott re-creates that gloating spirit; then, in the remaining lines (three each at the end of the penultimate and last verses) he deftly destroys it. Notice that the undercutting of that fantastical world (which the poet sees as sentimental and cruel – how do we know?) is achieved not merely by referring to the hawk by its English name, but by abrupt changes in the rhythm and tone of the poem. Attempt to analyse these.

Why (in v. 3) are the mouths 'slack'? What or whose 'limbs' are left shaking? Give two meanings of the first line of v. 4; what view of West Indian history is Walcott offering in 'Hawk'?

Consider that shadowy figure to which the hawk is compared: a grandee with extended hands 'waltzing alone,/alone, to the old

113

parang'. Does he escape the poet's condemnation? (Would you like him to? Why?)

Mass Man

In 'Hawk' Walcott indicts the Creole mentality and its revellers; in 'Mass Man' he defends (against their counterattack?) the role in society of the meditative man.

The poem opens with images of Carnival. Notice how, by describing the man-inhabited costumes as 'metaphors', the poet cannily implies a parallel between the masqueraders' activity and his own. Furthermore, 'coruscating' means glittering, but also 'brilliant in intelligence or wit'. Likewise, 'making style' (v. 2), a colloquialism translatable as 'showing off', has as its secondary meaning 'creating a style' or cultural mode (see also below). The revellers, whose 'hedonism is so sacred that to withdraw from it, not to jump up, to be a contemplative outside of its frenzy is a heresy' (Walcott, in 'On Choosing Port-of-Spain'), challenge the poet-heretic to join them. The poet's defence of his role as spectator-witness is threefold. He points to the existence of suffering in the midst of the carnival (that child who 'collapses, sobbing'); he claims identity with the revellers, reminding them of their common history of slavery and acknowledging his own 'mania' (as history's creation? Cf. *Another Life*: 'The dream/of reason had produced its monster:/a prodigy of the wrong age and colour'); and he asserts that 'someone' must bear witness to the tragic dimensions of life, must link the dancers to their past and inescapable future ('dust to dust'), and in this way give them back to themselves.

Mass Man: A pun. Carnival masqueraders are termed 'mas men'; but see also Walcott's description of Carnival as 'an exultation of the mass will'.

barges (v. 2, l. 2): Another pun. Cleopatra travelled down the Nile on a ceremonial barge.

making style (v. 2, l. 3): For Walcott's views on the function of mimicry in the creation of a culture, see his essay, 'The Caribbean: Culture or Mimicry?' or these lines, from 'The Schooner *Flight*': '. . . and we,/if we live like the names our masters please,/by careful mimicry might become men'.

'Join us,' they shout, 'O God, child, you can't dance?' (v. 2, l. 4): What gods and children share is an untrammelled capacity for joy. But the line is also an exact reproduction of colloquial Trinidadian. (Notice how 'dance', in dragging the last syllable of 'radiance' towards rhyme, ensures a Trinidadian pronunciation of the latter word.)

your penitential morning (v. 4, l. 1): Ash Wednesday, the first day of the Roman Catholic season of Lent. It follows immediately upon the two days of Carnival.

Landfall, Grenada

In 'Nearing Forty' Walcott relates how, as a poet, his 'life bled for/the household truth, the style past metaphor/that finds its parallels, however wretched,/in simple, shining lines . . .' 'Landfall, Grenada', in itself a minor elegy, exhibits that movement away from rhetoric (both verbal and emotional) and towards the age-old simplicities of 'true feeling' (Walcott: 'Winding Up'). Appropriately, the poem extols the virtue of reticence, and its language approaches that of prose. The rhymes are unobtrusive: either unstressed (heard/lowered, stars/mariners), or internal (ocean/motion, those/impose, ease/elegies), or the rhyme words are widely separated (place/race, offend/end). The syntax is straightforward, the cadences calm. Indeed, the poem tends towards silence – itself identified by the poet as a circumstance of death ('cannot be heard', 'climbs out of sound'). The exhortation of the last five lines may constitute an unwitting irony (the poem is itself a neat, gravestone elegy rhyming the dead man's end), and the odd surge of gallows humour ('rigidly anchored', 'Deep friend') threatens the tone of steady acceptance which the poet seeks and, in the main, achieves. The canes 'surging to cumuli' are presumably burning (though 'cumulus' has another, esoteric meaning, viz. accumulation). The line, 'your death was a log's entry', is prose. Consider the implications of 'tiered sea', 'ruled stars'.

Homecoming: Anse La Raye

And so one summer after I returned, we arranged
to stay in the old village, and we spent
two days and one night there, but except

115

for the first few hours it was somehow different,
as if either the island or myself had changed ...
and I left there that morning with a last look
at things that would not say what they once meant.
                              WALCOTT: *Another Life*

'Homecoming: Anse La Raye' re-creates that experience, of the loss of
one's sense of home. The poet, visiting the island of his birth, dis-
covers that 'there are no rites/for those who have returned'. The
landscape strikes him as desultory and as though war-torn; the chil-
dren, like the stunted survivors of a war, reveal the symptoms of
malnutrition. He finds that they mistake him for a tourist, a potential
source of money, and sees his earlier hope that 'it would mean
something to declare/today, I am your poet, yours', as having been
futile. The reference to 'homecomings without home' is of course
ironic; the actual experience is of arriving nowhere. Thus in the final
verse the poet feels 'dazed', and the real world seems forbidding,
alien. Ghosts occupy the shade under the palm trees.

Helen (v. 1, l. 3): Helen of Troy, in the *Iliad* and *Odyssey* the wife of
Menelaus. Her abduction by the Trojan Paris, who marries her,
causes war between the Trojans and the Greeks. After the war she is
successfully reconciled with her first husband and homeland. The
parallel lies in the notion of the poet also being married twice: first to
the island of his birth, and later to the muse of poetry, who leads him
abroad. The reference to Helen also prepares us for the battlefield
imagery of the succeeding lines.

the shades/of borrowed ancestors (v. 1, ll. 3–4): Anticipates the 'dead
fishermen' of the final verse, in a sense the poet's 'real' ancestors.

her looms (v. 1, l. 7): The overzealous listener may hear 'heirlooms', but
the phrase is obscure, unless Walcott is now referring to Penelope,
another of the *Odyssey*'s embattled wives, and a tireless weaver – see
note to 'Lampfall'.

drilled in our skulls (v. 1, l. 8): Force-fed us at school. But 'drilled' also
sustains the loom image.

Suffer them to come (v. 2, 1.1): Cf. Christ: 'Suffer little children to come
unto Me.' How appropriate is the poet's likening of his relationship
with the children to that of Christ's? (Is it ironic, do you think?)

116

your needle's eye (v. 2, l. 2): Christ taught that it was easier for a camel to pass through the eye of a needle than for a rich man to enter heaven.

reflecting nothing (v. 3, l. 8): (1) unthinking; (2) manifesting emptiness; (3) having no relationship with the environment. The phrase also echoes the earlier 'You give them nothing'. (Is the poet referring only to money, do you think?)

dead/fishermen . . . eating their islands (v. 3, ll. 14–16): An hallucination. The 'dazed' poet sees ghosts playing draughts with the West Indian islands, 'eating' them. The vision reflects the 'disappearance' of his sense of home. The reference to politicians is probably meant to direct our minds to the disintegration of the West Indies Federation, a collapse now widely attributed to self-seeking politicians 'playing politics' with the islands.

Cold Spring Harbour

'Cold Spring Harbour' evokes simultaneously two kinds of death. There is psychic death, the loss of hope: that 'dark child's' dreaming preparation for 'the white world of men' is shown to have been misconceived; the child's expectation of what lies beyond the 'door' (l. 10) is confounded in the man ('dumbstruck') when the door opens. And there is the poet's intimation of actual death: 'the strange violation . . . of perfect snow'. In the poem the two themes are interwoven and cannot really with coherence be unravelled (a triumph or weakness of the poem?); none the less, think if you can of two meanings of 'the white world of men', one applicable to each kind of death.

The poem develops between the poles of its parentheses (of which the first – syntactically implied – is, 'did/he know it was dark then'). Notice how our sense of the child's wonder, evoked mainly by the *w* sounds of ll. 7–9, gives way, with successive repetitions of the word 'white', to intimations of a blanker silence; and that 'What urges [him] towards this white,/snow-whipped wood' is – ominously – left unsaid. Consider also how resistant to true cadence (i.e. to respite) is the run-on tetrameter, the poem's main line.

Cold Spring Harbour is on Long Island, off the north-eastern seaboard of the United States. Given the poem's theme, however, what the significance of the name itself? Is the poet missing his children because they are not with him in the flesh? Or because they too are lost, as he was, in a dream of 'old Christmas card[s]?'.

'Cold Spring Harbour' is one of a number of poems in which Walcott refers to himself in the second person singular, in effect addressing himself. While this mannerism (which first appears in *The Gulf*) may be taken as symptomatic of the poet's loss of faith in the existence of an audience for his poetry, the impression on the reader is rather of a division, or gulf, arising between Walcott-the-poet and Walcott-the-man. The latter listens – and, presumably, obeys – as the former guides, admonishes, explains. In the present poem there is a third Walcott: the 'dark child' referred to as 'he'. Consider how much of its tension, its shrouded sense of disturbance and danger – which converges upon the lure of that 'white, snow-whipped wood' – 'Cold Spring Harbour' owes to the impression of dissociation which the existence of these three Walcotts conveys.

Love in the Valley

Though it may shine, bemuse or enchant, art is not life. What is living moves and changes; art stays still; and like memory it glazes its object. The world of art is a dream-world, its creatures spectral, its light winterish or submarine or stilly gold; and in that sense it is deathly: as silent – and as eternal – as death. 'Love in the Valley' re-creates the experience of entering the world of art (in this case, of literature): its wonder and drifting, dreamlike sequences, and also its silence.

Notice how Walcott persuades language into creating that aura of silence. While others have used the iambic trimeter to hurry a poem along (the hallmarks of this line are briskness and a clipped concision), Walcott uses it here to quite different effect. This he does (1) by allowing the line to dictate the cadence. Notice that virtually all the lines (with the exception of the last verse – why?) end either with unstressed syllables or with monosyllabic nouns, in each case causing the auditory imagination momentarily to linger. Thus the poem is full of – at times, barely perceptible – pauses, even where no punctuation occurs. (2) By *not* allowing (except, for dramatic reasons, 'heavy', v. 8 and 'literature', v. 16) any cadence to be too pronounced. There is a deliberate dearth of full stops, and in most cases the word upon which the period falls is soon picked up by rhyme. The combined effect of (1) and (2) is to defeat the speaking voice, which moves normally in broad

118

sweeps between pronounced cadences, and to cause the poem to be read either silently, or in a voice of quiet incantation; and this, given its theme, is also its main, and major, achievement.

The sun goes slowly blind (v. 1, l. 1): i.e. the material world fades.

the valley of the shadow (v. 1, l. 3): Cf. 'Yea, though I walk through the valley of the shadow of death, I will fear no evil, for Thou art with me . . .'

evening dims the mind (v. 2, l. 2): A variation of the first line, it indicates that while the journey about to be made may be rendered metaphorically in terms of the material world, it is in fact to be a journey of the imagination.

I shake my head in darkness (v. 2, l. 3): Secreting the image of a horse, this line prepares us for the head of Pasternak 'like a thaw-sniffing stallion' (v. 7).

leaden as eyes (v. 4, l. 1): In what state do eyes become leaden?

a skein of drifting hair (v. 4, l. 2): Appearing from nowhere, as things do in dreams? Or from the shaken head? Follow the path of that skein of hair; under what guises does it reappear?

the blank pages (v. 5, l. 1): Of the poet's workbook.

vertiginous (v. 5, l. 3): Causing dizziness and a sense of falling. Here, falling out of the material world and into the world of imagination, of art.

drift (v. 6, l. 1): Since the narrator is now disembodied. The 'I' is thus his imagination, not his corporeal self, and therefore . . .

through hostile images /of white and black, and look (v. 6, ll. 2–3): . . . the world becomes a child's wonderland ('and look').

thaw-sniffing (v. 7, l. 1): i.e. sensing the moment when winter breaks, and life resumes.

Pasternak (v. 7, l. 2): Boris Pasternak (1890–1960), Russian poet and novelist, awarded the Nobel Prize (which he refused) for his novel *Dr Zhivago* – a love story (whose heroine is called Lara, see v. 15, l. 3) set against the turmoil of revolutionary Russia.

the frozen spring (v. 8, l. 1): ... of passional life in post-revolutionary Russia. Pasternak was expelled from the Union of Soviet Writers for criticizing the Soviet system. The succeeding lines symbolize his death.

a white childhood (v. 9, l. 1): Because the world of imagination is conceived here as white? Or because the children's stories were usually set in a world of white people and of winter?

bracelets (v. 9, l. 2): Of frost.

Hawthorne's fairy book (v. 10, l. 3): Nathaniel Hawthorne (1804–64) was an American novelist who published a volume of stories for children entitled *The Tanglewood Tales*.

Hardy's (v. 12, l. 2): Thomas Hardy (1840–1928), English poet and novelist. His novels include *Tess of the D'Urbervilles* and *Far from the Madding Crowd*, in which the heroine is called Bathsheba (see v. 15).

hailstorms (v. 12, l. 3): Possibly a reference to the First World War. Hardy's work revealed a premonition of doom such as was realized by that war.

the depth of whiteness (v. 14, l. 3): Silence and death – see introductory paragraph to this note.

the numbing kiss (v. 15, l. 1): Their kiss is 'deathly' (cf. above) ...

whose tragedy ... love of literature (v. 16): ... and yet their fictional tragedies make real life by comparison seem mundane, and their love seems more vital than (my) love of fiction.

Nearing Forty

Two impulses contend in 'Nearing Forty'. There is the poet's lament for what he perceives as his failing powers, and there is his (compensatory?) affirmation – in support of which the quote from Johnson has clearly been adduced – of 'the household truth'.

The affirmation, to begin with, is tenuous. Bitterness and disgust threaten (consider the tone of 'which would be just', or the emphatic rhymes, 'wretched/stretched', 'gutter/sputter') and the poet becomes aware of the temptation to succumb to these, and thus to wind up sounding like 'the dry wheezing of a dented kettle'. Another approach occurs to him, however: to 'rise and set your lines to work/with sadder joy but steadier elation'; and though the poem announces no choice, its movement implies that Walcott will embrace the latter alternative, of acceptance and duty.

Thematically, 'Nearing Forty' is reminiscent of Wordsworth's 'Intimations of Immortality'. In particular, its final eight lines recall these of the latter poem:

> Though nothing can bring back the hour
> Of splendour in the grass, of glory in the flower,
> We will grieve not, rather find
> Strength in what remains behind ...
> In the faith that looks through death,
> In years that bring the philosophic mind.

And, like Wordsworth's poem, 'Nearing Forty' is 'rigidly-metred' and rhymed – an appropriate approach for a professional poet, one who feels his 'imagination ebb[ing]' but who is none the less determined to 'rise and set [his] lines to work'.

Is there a problem with all this, though? Does Walcott in fact view his work as 'a false dawn, fireless and average'? Does the fact that 'Nearing Forty' runs on, without losing coherence, for 32 lines without a full stop – except at the end – suggest the effort of a failing poet, or some kind of *tour de force*? (Look again at 'seems' in the final line.)

The Walk

Predominantly an evocation of the nervous exhaustion – like 'cold sweat fil[ing] from high tension wires' – which can afflict a writer after a hard day's work, 'The Walk' nonetheless attempts to affirm the bulwarks, of heart and home, which may restrain a man in such a state from an act of despair.

Under the influence of the poet's 'doubt' – really a malaise whose symptom is the 'brain that tires,/and loses faith' in the worth of its effort – the religious imagery of the opening lines gives way to images of illness. The poet sees himself as a patient who has spent the day 'prone, haemorrhaging' poems. Taking a stroll (like a convalescent?), he is struck by the way people ('cats') with the capacity to be free-ranging souls ('lions') none the less seem to prefer the boredom

121

('yawn') of being caged; then, finding himself instinctively turning back at the end of the street, he acknowledges his own heart's attachment, and finds awesome ('terrible') its fidelity, not only to home, but to life, i.e. its capacity to endure – which is why the poet praises it as a 'rose of iron'.

In a vacant lot the poet comes upon a bamboo grove through which a path 'hisses' – like a serpent (a visual image), but perhaps also like the tempter in paradise. The temptation, since 'Only the pain . . . is real', is to commit suicide; but in a startling image (final line), in which the houses are portrayed as having acquired the leonine qualities surrendered to them by their tenants, the poet discovers himself implacably restrained.

'The Walk' however achieves at best an inconclusive statement. The experience it imparts is of despair only tenuously held in check by the heart's capacity to endure and by the gravitational pull of home. In 'The Chelsea', written a decade later, when Walcott, in his late forties, had begun to wander the world, he writes of 'Happier lives,/settled in ruts, and great for wanting less'. On the evidence of 'The Walk', do you think he really believes this? In what tone would you declaim the exhortation, 'arise, stroll on . . .'? Do you find anything melodramatic about the utterance, 'Only the pain,/the pain is real' (and if so, what does this suggest about the pain?). How central to the poet's mood is the belief stated in ll. 17–19, and is this belief a cause or effect of that mood?

Re-read 'The Walk', interpreting 'you/your' as the poet's spirit, and the house as a house of flesh, i.e. his body. Can this interpretation be sustained? Does it enrich the poem?

Another Life, Extract A

The opening movement, it introduces the poem's main themes: West Indian history and the poet's own cultural ambivalence; the nature of imagination; the author's apprenticeship as a painter; and a landscape awaiting 'verification'. The extract also introduces two of the poem's three main characters (apart from the poet himself). The girl is 'Anna' (see Extracts F and G), the poet's first love; the master is Harold Simmons, the young Walcott's artistic guide, and the subject of the moving elegy which comprises Extract H.

122

Another Life, Extract B
Death, physical or psychic, shadows *Another Life* in many guises. The extract describes the child's first experience of death. The lantern-jawed gravekeeper will reappear, with the impact of a mythic character, at the end of the poem.

Another Life, Extract C
The 'heroes' are St Lucia's cast of 'characters', many of them eccentrics, described in previous chapters. The extract advances the notion of the identity of the religious and artistic impulses; describes a crucial experience in the adolescent's life; recalls the attraction for the young poet of the retreating 'ordered, colonial world'; declares that, for him, (another?) 'life began' when he fell in love with art – and then immediately brings nearer the figure of Anna, thus suggesting connections (though the poet also warns of contradictions) between the love of art and sexual love. The departure of the 'moonlit' liner, with which the chapter ends, premonishes other journeys – including the journey into the realm of imagination – and intimates also the poet's own eventual death.

Another Life, Extract D
introduces 'Gregorias' – the St Lucian painter Dunstan St Omer – the third major character of the poem, and describes the awakening 'golden' year of the two young painters, 'drunk' on their love of art and determined to chart, in paintings, the 'several postures' of their 'virginal' island. The extract captures the idealism, elation, wonder and self-assurance of late adolescence. The 'finished soldier' is St Omer's widowed father.

Another Life, Extract E
forewarning of a later, darker stage in the life of the artist, his youthful euphoria gone and nervous exhaustion threatening, the extract is informed by the mature Walcott's experience of subsequent 'deaths': the suicide of Simmons, the failure of Gregorias, the near-breakdown of the poet himself. It ends with a dramatic evocation of the great fire that razed most of Castries, the capital of St Lucia, in 1948.

Another Life, Extract F
Following Anna's soliloquy, that of a girl awaking to young woman-
hood, the chapter moves swiftly to an intimation of eventual separa-
tion and its recurring motifs: the walk/journey/voyage. It ends with a
majestic sonnet exploring the contradictory demands of spirit and
flesh, divine and human love ('in time' means in due course; but also
'in the temporal world' – which art transcends).

Another Life, Extract G
Describes the merging, in the young poet's imagination, of 'his' Anna
with the Annas of literature (in particular, the heroine of Pasternak's
Dr Zhivago) – an act of possession which none the less constitutes an
unwitting denial of the uniqueness of the real Anna, who (partly in
consequence?) soon leaves the island to study nursing in England.
The extract represents a feat of sustained and passionate lyricism
without parallel (to this annotator's knowledge) in English language
twentieth-century poetry.

Another Life, Extract H
Following the poet's discovery that Harold Simmons has killed him-
self, this extract comprises Walcott's elegy for his former tutor. I
expresses a reverential notion of the relationship between the artis
and his community: Simmons becomes 'a man no more/but the fer
vour and intelligence/of a whole country'.

Another Life, Extract I
Argues the primacy of the creative imagination, and its capacity bot
to possess and to transcend the events of history. (See Walcott'
essay: 'The Muse of History'.)

Another Life, Extract J
The conclusion of the poem. In it Walcott asserts, with a rather forlo
defiance ('And what if . . .?'), the enduring power of Imagination ('t
moon/will always swing its lantern') in the face of general destructi

(specifically, of the island's landscape, but one recalls the poem's other 'deaths'); asks forgiveness of the folk; confronts again the spectre of the old gravekeeper; bids farewell to Gregorias and Anna – and then, as if reluctant to let the poem end here, resurrects Gregorias to recall (as Othello, at the last, recalls his greatest triumphs) the mood and achievements of their 'golden year'. The gesture seems one of defiance. The last line of the poem is disturbingly private. (In fact, both names were the poet's nicknames for St Omer.)

The Virgins
Though Frederiksted is in the Virgin Islands, the title is of course ironic; the poem is a wry, and in places bitter reflection on the ways in which tourism can destroy the culture of a small and predominantly rural community. Its chief delights are to be found in its compression of meaning, its controlled and certain tone, its relentless evocation of vacuity, and – assaulting this last – the ingenious and 'vigorous' metaphor with which it ends.

the dead streets (l. 1): Dead because (1) it is the hottest time of day; (2) some rumour of impending civil unrest has driven the tourists away for the time being; (3) tourism has 'killed' the island's culture.

sun-stoned (l.1): (1) pelted by the sun; (2) dazed, as with sunstroke.

free port (l. 2): Where certain taxes have been lifted in order to attract commerce. But in context the term also refers to the original port (i.e. harbour or home) of the island's once 'free' inhabitants.

at funeral pace (l. 3): Why?

of life not lost to the American dream (l. 4): i.e. 'of a time when life in the islands had not yet been corrupted by the American dream of afflu-nce'. Likewise, ll. 6–8.

civilized (l. 6): Ironically contrasted with 'simplicities'. Walcott is of course upholding the latter against the former.

for the good life . . . on the rise (ll. 8–9): Meaning (roughly): these islands sell their few assets (of climate and coast) so cheaply that their economies remain stagnant, increasing the numbers of the un-mployed, who in desperation turn to crime.

125

blighted (l. 10): The sun brings the tourists and tourism destroys; thus the sun is a blight.

blown dry by the hysteria (l. 11): Notice the cry of the wind in '*hys*teria'.

A condominium drowns/in vacancy (ll. 12–13): Try to imagine *how* that condominium 'drowns' in 'vacancy'.

jewelled (l. 14): Descriptive of a housefly in the sun. But Walcott also intends us to think of the stereotype of the bejewelled American matron.

by revving up . . . banks of silver thresh (ll. 18–19): The image is of local craft collecting and ferrying tourists to the casinos and banks. But of course those 'banks of silver' are not only the commercial banks 'thresh[ing]' their harvests of profits, but also underwater banks of fish. Walcott thus manages to suggest the past and present in a phrase, and to imply the destruction of the livelihood of the locals (fishing) by the advent of tourism.

Adam's Song

The notion behind 'Adam's Song' is that the Word made Flesh ceases to be the Word – that while divine love assures immortality, profane love humanizes us and, thus, commits us eventually to die. So, when Adam sings 'the song to Eve' he does so 'at the price/of his own death' and in fear 'of the jealousy of God'. Yet the poet clearly sides with Adam, whom he presents as a brave, doomed – but above all, human – figure. 'Adam's Song' asserts the essential tragedy (but also the poignancy – witness the ineffable tenderness of the song) of the human condition.

The adulteress stoned to death (v. 1, l. 1): Christ halted a mob intent on stoning an adulteress to death by insisting that the first stone should be thrown by someone 'without sin'.

that films her flesh with slime (v. 1, l. 4): Both the imagery and the sound of the line recall the serpent. The implication is that malicious gossip are like the devil.

horned God (v. 2, l. 2): Horned means betrayed. But the devil is also popularly depicted with horns, i.e. as 'a horned God'. In this sense 'for' means 'for an image of'.

the song to Eve/against his own damnation (v. 4, ll. 1–2): 'Against': (1) 'in defiance of', i.e. even at the price of; (2) 'as proof against'. The lines thus compose this paradox: that human love, which condemns us to die, is also our salvation. (Do you see any connection between this and the American poet Robert Lowell's affirmation of 'man's lovely/ peculiar power to choose life and die'?)

with the lights . . . kingdom (v. 5, ll. 1–2): The lights are coming on in the panthers' eyes because darkness is falling (and cats can see in the dark). But the image is also of an incipient attack. The panthers are in this sense God's avengers, 'coming out of the trees' towards Adam.

the jealousy of God (v. 6, l. 2): Like that of a jilted lover. In fact the Old Testament God is often portrayed as jealous, temperamental and wrathful.

The song ascends to God, who wipes his eyes (v. 7): God hears Adam's song, and stops weeping. Why, do you think?

Heart . . . the dew is (v. 8, ll. 1–3): The word 'Heart' at the beginning of each of these lines is Adam's term of endearment for Eve.

Parades, Parades

In this poem Walcott scathingly indicts one of the post-Independence West Indian governments – a government which he views as uncreative and gluttonous, and thus inherently totalitarian.

'Parades, Parades' opens in a tone of mixed bemusement and indignation. (Notice that the opening line seems to fade into air, suggesting: tiredness? bewilderment? vacancy? How is this effect achieved?) Independence has opened up horizons – desert, ocean, sky – but the old iniquities remain, while the politicians 'plod/without imagination', so that the fountain of creative action remains dry. Lines 5–7 are imprecise: their meaning seems to be that the jets scratch the same lines, or trails, in the blue sky above the mountains.) In the repetition of 'same' – 'the same lines . . . the same steps' – Walcott's bemusement gives way to irritation, and he declares the Governor-General a 'fool'. (Why, do you think?)

In the second verse the poet describes a more sinister aspect of the Independence Day parades. He watches the 'eyes of the beauti-ul/and unmarked children' from the countryside 'widen in terror' of the nationalistic sentiments being thundered at them, and is moved to consider the heretical notion that nationalism may be evil – that perhaps life was 'truer' in the colonial days, when 'the law lived far away' (and, being remote, might also have been impersonal?). In fact, the impulse behind these lines is the conservative belief that the people of a country have a right not to be harangued by the State.

In the final verse the political circus appears: Papa (Papa Doc was the nickname of the despotic ruler of Haiti) and his 'sleek, waddling seals ... trundling up to the dais'. (Notice how 'sleek' suggests slyness, and 'waddling' both gluttony and gracelessness. Is there a sense, do you think, in which contemptuous laughter, like Walcott's here, can destroy its object?) The wind, symbol of 'inspiration', puts its tail between its legs. Note how, as the crowd falls suddenly silent, the poem itself stops 'abruptly'. (How does Walcott create that decisive cadence?)

The ensuing questions are rhetorical. We know that the silence is not one of respect but of unease; that the 'hoarse hosannas' (why the religious term, do you think?) represent 'awe' only in its debased sense of fear (they were 'forced'); and that the poet's conception of a 'New World' of the spirit is a far cry from the 'tin-ringing tune' of those 'pumping, circling horns'.

To whom is the poet speaking in the last five lines of the poem? Is his demand, 'Tell me ... why I said nothing', really a confession of complicity, that he remained silent when he should have spoken up in protest? Or a further indictment of the regime, that in its presence (from which even the wind flees) poetry is not possible? (Cf. W. B Yeats, in 'A Model for the Laureate': 'The muse is mute when public men/Applaud a modern throne:/Those cheers that can be bought or sold,/That office fools have run ...') What name would you be inclined to give to 'that look on the faces/of the electorate'?

The Wind in the Dooryard

Eric Roach, to whom this poem is dedicated, was a Tobagonian poet (b. 1914) who committed suicide in 1974. In his poetry he celebrated the life of the village, those rural communities of peasants and fishermen of African origin now modishly referred to as 'the folk'. He reported to have been deeply disillusioned by the break-up of the West Indies Federation, which, like Walcott (see 'Homecoming: An

La Raye') he attributed to the ambitions of individual politicians – and which appears to have coincided with the beginning of Roach's pre-occupation with his own death, a preoccupation which progressively became obsessive. In his last years he waged a brief but bitter (if eventually futile) battle against the breakdown of literary standards in the islands, as evinced by a rash of publications of mostly worthless verse – publications which were nonetheless championed by certain academics as heralding a breakthrough of the oral tradition into scribal literature, and as sociologically relevant. Roach was for many years Agriculture Reporter for the *Trinidad Guardian*.

'The Wind in the Dooryard' shares with 'Parades, Parades' a certain informality of construction. In both Walcott eschews metre, and the tingling near-approach to metre which characterizes some of his most successful poems, and relies instead upon his ear for the natural cadences of the speaking voice. This is of course the method of *vers libre*, but without a sure organic movement of the whole poem it becomes an alibi for the inclusion of anything. 'The Wind in the Dooryard' seems – as 'Parades, Parades' does not – to transgress the boundary between flexibility and formlessness. (One suspects, for example, that the shape of the poem would be modified hardly at all by omitting the whole of the eighth verse – or by adding, here and here, a number of one-line descriptive clauses.) The student of poetry might do well to consider here the air of *inevitability* which characterizes a good poem. To what extent does the repetition of 'I didn't want . . . I did not want' temper the sensation of arbitrariness which the form of the poem exudes?

Dooryard: The (often dirt) yard outside the door of a house or shack. But the term is almost certainly meant to bring to mind Walt Whitman's great elegy for the assassinated American President, Abraham Lincoln: 'When Lilacs Last in the Dooryard Bloom'd'.

salt (v. 1, l. 4): Embittered; but also, 'salted by the sea'. While it was later discovered that Roach had taken poison and thrown himself from a cliff, the news that his body had been found at Quinan Bay (on the south-east coast of Trinidad) led most people initially to believe that he had drowned himself by swimming out to sea. 'The Wind in the Dooryard' (see also ll. 17–20) exhibits this misapprehension – as does at least one other poem on the subject written soon after Roach's death.

what he celebrated (v. 2): Notice that Walcott's poem, while dedicated to a man who finally turned his back on life, is itself a celebration of life – an implicit disavowal of Roach's last action. Thus, rather than being a lament about death, the poem is, rather, a testament to the implacable surge of life (note that the sunrise, v. 5, 'force[s]' the sleeper to awake); a lifeforce which, Walcott asserts, Roach once recognized, and affirmed, in the rhythms and activities of the country.

his rusty theme (v. 7. l. 4): Can you think of three reasons (apart from the suggestion of 'rustic') why Walcott refers to Roach's theme as 'rusty'?

Shango (v. 7, l. 6): Yoruba god of thunder and fertility.

The Bright Field
In 'The Bright Field' Walcott returns to and develops the theme of the much earlier 'Ruins of a Great House', the common destiny of colonist and colonized. The poems are also worth comparing in terms of language. Notice how, in the fifteen or more years which separate them, the voice inhabiting the pentameter has grown markedly less mellifluous, less declamatory, and more flexible: in short, more open to the movement of intelligence. Analyse the ways in which the two poems employ metre and rhyme. To what extent does your analysis throw light upon the ways in which this change of tone has been achieved?

the sense/we all have (v. 1, ll. 2–3): The first gesture of inclusion. London and the Caribbean are further linked, both explicitly (in 'cane or wheat', 'cab [and] bullock-cart', 'lanes or cane fields') and by simile ('like dark canes, the river spires') and metaphor (the 'pool of London', [The Thames] i.e. like the bay of Salybia). See also the parallel between swallows and pelicans in the final verse.

self-defence (v. 1, l. 4): Against the civilization of the former colonist. But they also, living in London, must employ self-defence, since 'selves' (l. 6) are 'humbled [i.e. feel threatened] by massive places'.

who moved ... was moved (v. 1, ll. 7–8): Who once moved in anger . was moved to pity. (Cf. 'Ruins of a Great House': 'All in compassion ends'. Also, 'The Harbour': 'Time knows that bitter and sly sea'.)

Underground-bound (v. 1, l. 8): Headed for (1) the subway, (2) the grave.

Their sun that would not set was going down (v. 2, l. 1): Like other imperial nations, Britain once harboured the hope that 'the sun would never set' on its empire; i.e. that the empire would endure for ever. Walcott's line is an ironic comment on that hope; but in the context of the poem it is also a reminder of mortality.

with the compassion of calendar art (v. 2, l. 4): Art may conceivably be termed compassionate because it immobilizes scenes, preserving them from time, and thus from death. Calendar art, however, is meant to endure for a specific time only, before the page is turned. It is unclear whether Walcott means us to see compassion in the fact that the depicted scene is preserved at all, even for a short time, or in the swiftness and painlessness with which it is banished.

like walking sheaves of harvest (v. 2, l. 5): Night is the harvester. It gains support as a metaphor for death from that antithetical 'quick' in the same line.

the loud belt (v. 2, l. 8): Walcott likens the street to a conveyor belt. The implication is that the inhabitants of great cities are reduced by them to component parts in a factory (see note on 'self-defence').

feels . . . everything (v. 2, ll. 14–15): The passage from Donne quoted in the notes to 'Ruins of a Great House' ends: 'And therefore never send to know for whom the bell tolls; it tolls for thee.'

original sin (v. 2, l. 16): In Christian religions original sin brought the knowledge of good and evil into the world, destroying Paradise and initiating history. London (i.e. the British) is here credited with (or accused of) having destroyed the 'paradisal' islands, and initiating West Indian history.

Samuel Palmer (v. 3, l. 1): English eighteenth-century engraver. In *Another Life* Walcott quotes Yeats's reference to twilight as 'the lonely light that Samuel Palmer engraved'.

Blake's (v. 3, l. 2): William Blake, English poet, painter and prophetic visionary, was a contemporary of Palmer's. Believing in the possibility of building a new 'Jerusalem' in 'England's green and pleasant land', he was enraged by the sordid effects of the early industrial revolution on the English people and landscape. Why do you think Walcott focuses here on that pivotal moment in English culture?

These slow . . . rooks (v. 3, ll. 4–6): The belfry-strokes are imagined as stones thrown into a pool, the swallows as their concentric ripples. They function also as concretizations of that 'involuntary bell' which the heart feels.

across Salybia as the tide lowers (v. 3, l. 8): Notice how, like the poem and the belfry-strokes themselves, 'lowers' dies away.

Dark August

'Dark August' turns on its parenthetical lament (penultimate verse), in which 'they' refers to society – cf. those 'gossiping mosquitoes'. The poet's love is adulterous or in some other way considered anti-social. On account of it 'Everything goes to hell'.

'Dark August' thus belongs to that most populous family of poems – added to by every age, in every nation – singing of love embattled or thwarted. Where it differs from most of its companion pieces is in its conclusion; in the poet's determination to 'learn to love black days like bright ones'. (Does 'to love' have here any more emphatic meaning than 'to accept'? Can you think of a sense in which it is possible to love sorrow?)

Notice that while 'the dark days, the steaming hills' (echoed later by 'the black rain, the white hills') is an evocation of grief, the word 'rain', wherever in the poem it appears, stands rather for passion. ('Fixing', v. 4, is in this sense a veterinary term, meaning 'de-sexing'.) What connections does the poet suggest between passion and grief? How successful do you find the personification, 'My sister, the sun'? (Do you find daunting, for example, the leap of imagination necessary to conceive of the sun as having a 'forehead of flowers and eyes of forgiveness'?)

In this poem, only two words fully rhyme. Which are they? What term describes the relationship between 'ones' and 'once'?

Sea Canes

In 'Frederiksted, Dusk', Walcott writes of the existence of 'something between life/and death' (notice, incidentally, the artful delineation –

as if that 'something's habitat was the small pause between the lines).

This 'something' is not identified. In fact it seems to be as mysterious, as ultimately unnameable, as Wordsworth's 'something far more deeply interfused ... a motion ... a spirit ...', though Walcott appears to conceive of it rather as a species of light. (In 'Frederiksted, Dusk' he refers to it as 'Whatever it is/that leaves bright flesh like sand and turns it chill', and observes that it 'would shine in them'.)

In 'Sea Canes' this 'something' is again alluded to. We learn that it is 'stronger' than lost love; that it has 'the rational radiance of stone'; that it goes (or lies) 'further than [or beyond] despair'; that it is 'strong as the wind' – and that it is capable of bringing 'those we love before us [just] as they were'. Its main attribute thus seems an ability to create an intense, emotionless realism, in defiance of time and death. Since the poet himself cannot name this 'something' (whatever it is) it is unlikely that we, his readers, should be able to. None the less, the student who is prepared to say something like 'I feel I know what he means but I can't describe it', should attempt to go further. (Is it an objective phenomenon? A state of mind? Imagination? Memory? Then, what is it?)

'Sea Canes' employs two distinct metres. The first four verses are predominantly trimetrical (producing an effect of – sadness? terseness? barely controlled emotion?) after which the lines lengthen into pentameters (suggesting – resignation? comprehension? peace?). Notice that the sixth line, rewritten as 'from the surf's faint drone', loses in effect – why? 'Green and silver' (l. 14) may imply daylight and moonlight (i.e. life and death) but as a visual image in the setting of the poem it is problematic (is the colour green discernible by moonlight?).

with faults and all, I cried (v. 1, l. 4): Do you find jarring the dissonance (after 'dead', 'earth', 'instead') of 'cried'? If so, do you think the dissonance was intended, or is a flaw of the poem?

snatch their talk (v. 2, l. 1): Assume that the poet began the line with the phrase 'snatches of conversation' in mind, then changed the first noun into a verb. What light does this throw on the nature of the poetic imagination?

surf's (v. 2, l. 2): What 'surf', precisely?

I cannot walk . . . earth's load (v. 2, l. 3 – v. 4, l. 1): These lines describe the disembodied souls of the dead in the act of leaving earth.

The sea-canes by the cliff flash green and silver (v. 5, l. 1): Look up, in connection with this line, the meaning of 'animism'.

enduring moonlight (v. 6, l. 2): Capable of enduring the light (or presence) of death (see note to 'The Schooner *Flight*').

Oddjob, a Bull Terrier

'Oddjob' was the name of a dog belonging to friends of Walcott. The poem describes the day of its dying: a darkening day, with rain coming and 'the gold [of sunlight] going out of the palms'. (Cf. Walcott's reference, in 'Frederiksted, Dusk', to 'Whatever it is/that leaves bright flesh like sand and turns it chill'.) The fading of light from the external world thus parallels (or is an 'objective correlative' of) the fading of life in the dog. The poet is struck by the owners' unpreparedness for their pet's death – by the fact that no one connected 'the fleck of the drizzle . . . with the dog's whimper' – an unpreparedness which, Walcott reflects, was in part due to the animal's inability to communicate: 'what follows at your feet/is trying to tell you/the silence is all'. (But consider that 'what follows' is not merely the dying dog but, in a wider, human sense, death itself.) With this reflection the poem arrives at its theme, which is silence; not only 'the silence of the dead' but also 'the silence of the deepest buried love' (a pun on 'buried'). The poet affirms that to be 'stricken dumb' is to be stricken 'deep' – that the profoundest emotions are 'unutterable/[yet] must be said'.

This reverence for silence, on the part of one whose preoccupation as a poet is first and foremost with language, is not paradoxical. Rather, Walcott is here acknowledging silence as the matrix of poetry, the brimming hinterland of emotion from which poetry issues. Can you think of a sense in which the silence of love – i.e. a love endured in silence – is 'blest/deepest by loss'? Is the tone of the last line one of grief, or wonder, or affirmation – or a combination of these?

One often comes across poems whose language overreaches their emotional content. 'Oddjob, A Bull Terrier' is the converse: a moving poem of great simplicity of expression. Consider the predominance of short or end-stopped lines, and the appropriateness of this to a poem whose theme is silence, or the power of silence. Is there a causal connection between the poem's ability to move us and the simplicity of its language?

Earth

It has been said – usually as a warning or rallying cry in a political context – that those who have nothing have nothing to lose. In 'Earth' Walcott takes this maxim and offers it as a source of solace and strength to someone in danger of emotional or psychic destitution. The poet, however, modifies the maxim. Those who have nothing else, he implies, still retain their connection with the earth, and, in an act of imitation so fervent that the poem describes it as a metamorphosis, can learn earth's stoicism (see, in connection, 'The Flock' – or, for a contrary view, the narrator's lament, in Chapter 5 of V. S. Naipaul's *The Mimic Men*, at 'the lack of sympathy between man and the earth he walks on').

'Earth' exhibits an intensity and a spareness which together convey the impression of urgency, turning the reader's concerned attention to the (unnamed) imperilled man or woman whom the poet is addressing, and giving the poem its dramatic force. As contributing to that air of urgency, consider (1) the poem's monolithic imagery; (2) its emphatic (because they begin their lines) exhortations: 'Let', 'feel', 'Sleep'; (3) the slow-burning hypnotist's voice behind the repeated 'You have never possessed anything . . . This is all you have owned . . .'

In the volume *Sea Grapes* 'Earth' follows immediately upon 'Odd-job, a Bull Terrier'. Does this fact seem significant?

To Return to the Trees

A poem concerned with the approach of old age, and the spectre of death which it brings, 'To Return to the Trees' affirms the need for a stoicism 'beyond joy [or] lyrical utterance'. Its heart lies in the significances imparted to the colour grey, in lines which constitute the poem's main achievement, since we are persuaded by them (and by that lovely easing of pace in the last verse) that the poet – and thus, by extension, the reader – is capable of confronting death with 'a heart at peace'.

135

Senex (v. 1, l. 1): Latin for 'old man'.

unwincing (v. 1, l. 3): Sounds the key note of the poem, and looks forward to 'stoic' and 'obdurate'.

geriatric (v. 2, l. 1): Ageing, or aged.

Cumana (v. 2, l. 2): A small town on the north-east coast of Trinidad.

To return to the trees (v. 2, l. 3): (1) To seek solace in the trees' capacity to endure; (2) to die, be buried, decompose, and thus become one with the tree-producing soil.

to decline (v. 3, l. 1): To fall. But the term also registers a schoolboy's 'laborious' declensions of Seneca's Latin (v. 15).

Ben Jonson (v. 3, l. 3): Elizabethan poet and playwright. Boanerges was his nickname.

lying (v. 4, l. 1): A (rather heavy-handed) pun: lying down/telling a lie.

gnarled (v. 5, l. 1): Like Seneca's 'gnarled' Latin, and (implicitly) the gnarled trunk of the 'felled almond'.

bearded with the whirlwind (v. 5, l. 2): Like certain pictorial representations (e.g. Blake's) of the Old Testament God (?).

flagrant (v. 7, l. 1): Flaming. Note that the meditation on grey grows out of the poet's observation of the day's 'ashen end'.

as it bestrides factions (v. 11, l. 3): Since it embraces both sides of a dispute. The notion is of an infinite capacity for acceptance.

Samson's (v. 12, l. 3): In the Bible, Samson was a judge of Israel famed for his strength. After many tribulations (he was seduced and betrayed by Delilah to the Philistines, who put out his eyes), he destroyed his captors' temple by pushing over its supporting pillars.

Atlas (v. 14, l. 2): In Greek mythology the Titan responsible for guarding the pillars of heaven (notice the train of thought *en route* from Samson), he was originally credited with holding up the sky (not 'the world', as in later representations, including Walcott's).

Seneca (v. 15, l. 2): Roman contemporary of Christ's, he was, among many things (orator, diplomat, financier), a playwright whose tragedies tended to suffer from verbosity – hence, 'that fabled bore'.

its two eyes (v. 17, l. 2): The pair of 'e's in 'eye', each of which contains an aperture or 'eye'.

this obdurate . . . slowly (v. 18, l. 3 – v. 19, l. 2): In another poem Walcott writes of the poet sinking 'to lose [his]name', and becoming the 'muscle shouldering the grass/through ordinary earth'.

Sabbaths, WI

'Sabbaths, WI' is an evocation of the 'melancholia' of small-island Sundays, thirty or forty years ago: the empty streets, the silent landscape, the old men playing draughts under the sea-almonds, the adults 'resting' after lunch, the revivalists gathering at dusk, on the horizon the tourist ships passing . . .

Comprised wholly of introductory clauses, the poem depends upon repetition and intonation to complete the sense of the sentence which it withholds (something like: 'pass before the mind's eye now'). Notice how the whole poem converges upon the line 'Those Sundays, those Sundays' – a line which composes its strenuous rhythms and webs its disparate images. After it, 'the engine of the sea' (*Another Life*) only seems to begin again; in fact the poem musingly dies away.

What is the effect of the lack of punctuation? The emotion concentrated in the line quoted above? The significance of the last line?

Forest of Europe

Joseph Brodsky, to whom the poem is dedicated, is an exiled poet from Soviet Europe living in the United States. 'Forest of Europe' has as its main setting the 'brown cottage' which Walcott, while teaching poetry in the USA (and thus a temporary 'exile' himself) shared with him for part of an Oklahoman winter.

The poem begins (and ends) with evocations of a winter forest whose location, appropriately, might equally be America or Europe. Winter has traditionally appeared in literature as a metaphor for exile (why, do you think?) and, between its opening and closing stanzas, 'Forest of Europe' explores that condition. The poem moves from the memory of Osip Mandelstam (see below) to the parallel experience of the American Indian (vv. 4–5) and then, via a reflection upon the cyclical nature of life (v. 6) to the great migrations of refugees from Soviet Europe and their archetypal experience: the journey of departure. With the reference to Brodsky's exiled compatriots as 'citizens of a language that is now yours', 'Forest of Europe' begins its own (counter-) movement, of affirmation. Poetry will survive persecution (v. 13, l. 2) as it survives the seasonal changes of earth (v. 13, l. 5), since it is the language of God (v. 15) – or of the indestructible urge towards self-expression (even the primates 'grunt').

Not the least of Walcott's claims upon our attention is this fact: that in an age that treats poetry as marginal, tolerating it (more or less) as a series of whimsical footnotes to a dour text co-authored by technologists and ideologues, he remains one of a very few poets writing in English who have steadfastly refused that trivializing notion of their function, insisting rather that the writing of poetry is a serious (not 'solemn') and ennobling exercise, calling for long, ardent apprenticeship, engaging the whole man, and capable of dealing with any aspect of human experience. 'Forest of Europe' is a major (arguably, a great) poem – multi-layered, unified, unclouded in perception, thematically epic and sure of tone – which could not have been composed by a poet used to approaching his task in any other spirit.

The last leaves . . . ear (v. 1, ll. 1–2): Can you imagine a sense in which the notes from a piano might resemble 'ovals' (or vowels)? The falling leaves are likened to musical notes; but in v. 13 the poet asserts that the 'music [of poetry] will last longer than the leaves'.

gawky music stands (v. 1, l. 3): The trees resemble music stands (1) visually, since their branches are bare; (2) because their leaves fell like musical notes ('notes' having in the meantime taken on the meaning of annotated music sheets).

manuscripts of snow (v. 1, l. 5): Pages of writing are throughout the poem likened to snow – cf. vv. 5 and 6. The snow is 'scattered' like the music sheets/musical notes/leaves.

the wintry breath (v. 2, l. 3): (1) because Brodsky is reciting the poem in winter; (2) because Mandelstam was deported by the Soviets to the frozen wastes of Asia, where he died; (3) because the lines themselves premonish (see note to v. 3, l. 1) the winter of exile.

Mandelstam (v. 2, l. 4): Osip Mandelstam was a lyric poet, born in Poland, who lived and published in the Soviet Union. For maintaining his independence from Stalinism he was persecuted and driven into exile. The date of his death has been kept secret by the Soviets, but is believed to be in 1940.

The rustling ... Neva (v. 3, l. 1): actually, 'The rustling of hundred-rouble notes above the lemon Neva.' The line is from Mandelstam's 'I Was Like a Child', which begins: 'I was like a child in that world of sovereign power/... and spiritually owe nothing to that world,/save that I may have suffered in the semblance of others.' The river Neva emerges into the sea at what is now Leningrad. Notice the evolution of the poem's opening image into that of Mandelstam's.

barren Oklahoma (v. 3, l. 5): Oklahoma, one of the American States, is described as barren because (1) it is in fact largely so, containing part of the eastern slope of the Rocky Mountains; (2) the time is winter; (3) to the two exiles it is not home.

Gulag Archipelago (v. 4, l. 1): Alexander Solzhenitsyn, a dissident Russian writer, was imprisoned and later expelled by the Soviets. (His fate thus resembles Mandelstam's.) In *The Gulag Archipelago* he describes the vast system of concentration camps for political dissidents which grew up under Stalin, and has survived him.

under this ice (v. 4, l. 2): i.e. buried in the American past.

the long Trail of Tears (v. 4, l. 3): Refers to the forced migrations of American Indians before the waves of colonists of European ancestry.

Choctaw ... treaties and white papers (v. 5, ll. 3–4): The Choctaw, an Indian tribe, signed treaties with the American Government but were none the less cheated out of their ancestral lands in present-day Alabama and Louisiana (white papers: Government edicts). The verse indicts the tendency of Movements (even those which begin with good intentions) to sacrifice, as they gather momentum, the 'single human' in the name of the Cause. Its placement in the poem implies that it is this tendency which is responsible for the creation of refugees and exiles.

one mind (v. 6, l. 4): Mandelstam's/Brodsky's.

the forest's tortured icons (v. 7, l. 1): In terms of the train journey, the winter trees. In terms of a journey of the imagination, artists incarcerated in 'forests' of concentration camps by totalitarian States. (Icons are sacred images of Eastern Christianity.)

the spires /of frozen tears (v. 7, ll. 2–3): Like stalagmites (?); cf. the 'salt, mineral spring' (v. 4, l. 2).

space /so desolate it mocked destinations (v. 8, ll. 4–5): Consider 'Forest of Europe' as a parable of the human condition – of the soul's journey through life. How is the phrase illumined by this interpretation of the poem?

that dark child (v. 9, l. 1): The young Brodsky. What is the expression on his face as he watches the river mint 'sovereigns stamped with power, not with poets'?

sovereigns (v. 9, l. 3): Coins – a visual image of light on unstill water; (2) rulers. In this sense the line refers to the growth of totalitarian regimes.

tributary (v. 10, l. 3): A branch of a river; but note the echoes of 'tribute' and 'tribulation'.

my South (v. 12, l. 1): The Caribbean.

there is no harder prison than writing verse (v. 12, l. 3): Because the writing of poetry (including 'free verse') involves submission to the dictates of form. The line, though it may be heartfelt, is of course an overstatement.

when, in his forest of barbed-wire branches (v. 13, l. 3): Notice that the forest of Europe has evolved from stands of trees to concentration camps.

Borealis . . . Archangel (v. 14, ll. 3–4): The Aurora Borealis is a luminous atmospheric phenomenon occurring near the earth's magnetic poles and visible from time to time by night. The image is of a peacock's tail, the extremities of its fan extending like callipers from Los Angeles in the USA to Archangel in the USSR. The verse affirms that poetry will live as long as earth itself. There is a secondary meaning, however. Boreas was the Greek god of the north wind, and 'boreal' means frosty or wintry. Borealis may thus be rendered as 'the hand of winter' – in the context of the poem, the creators of exile (i.e. totalitarian governments). Thus memory will need 'nothing to repeat', since exiles live on memories, and there will be then no exiles.

heavier than a boundary stone (v. 15, l. 4): Echoes v. 7, l. 5. The verse affirms the heroism of Mandelstam, who imprisoned, frightened, starved (and ill?), none the less went on writing poetry, itself an exhausting occupation.

as we grunt . . . cave (v. 16, ll. 2–3): Walcott affirms the identity of impulse which lies behind the poetry of modern writers like Brodsky and himself, and the first grunting approximate speech of man's ancestors. The implication is that speech as self-expression has always existed in human history and (by extension) always will. Note that Mandelstam's 'divine fever' produced a poem which, like an eternal flame, 'warms' (i.e. keeps alive the spirit of) other, latter-day exiles.

mastodons (v. 16, l. 5): The giant ancestors (now extinct) of the elephant. Walcott uses them here as a metaphor of States enforcing their ideological systems; the image contains the parallel prophecy of the eventual extinction of such regimes.

The Schooner *Flight*, Chapter 11 (After the Storm)

In 'The Harbour' the young poet/navigator began his 'progress outward/on a sea which is crueller than any word/of love'. Three decades on, 'The Schooner *Flight*' describes the experience of that voyage.

The poem's narrator and central character is Shabine ('the patois for/any red nigger'), a poet and occasional seaman. In the opening chapters he gives his reasons for quitting Trinidad, his homeland: (1) he was broke; (2) the corruption and materialism all around him had begun to 'poison [his] soul'; (3) he had been used (and then discarded) by a 'big government man' to smuggle Scotch – and now a Commission of Inquiry into smuggling was being set up; (4) he was quarrelling with his mistress, Maria Concepcion – quarrels which were 'mashing up my house and my family'. To escape all these (and after a mental breakdown which lands him in the lunatic asylum), he decides to enlist as a seaman on the inter-island schooner, *Flight*. This movement of the poem ends with Shabine's lament: 'Where is my rest place, Jesus? Where is my harbour?'

The ensuing chapters describe his real and imagined experiences (including an hallucination of the fleets and slaveships of history, and the *Flight*'s survival of a primal storm) on the voyage north.

Initially a simple narrative, 'The Schooner *Flight*' progressively and subtly emerges as an allegory of the journey of the poet's soul through life. That journey begins with the poet turning his back upon the loves and griefs of human society (though the memory of Maria Concepcion continues to haunt him like the ever-sought, never-possessed Muse of poetry – notice that her name echoes Catholicism's 'Muse': Mary of the Immaculate Conception). It leads him through the triumphs and travails of a life dedicated to poetry; until, in the final chapter (which comprises the present extract) he is granted a premonition of his own eventual end, as the light of literature merges with that of death to become 'a road in white moonlight taking me home'.

Though Walcott has not quite been able to overcome a certain tension inherent between Shabine the narrator (poet and contemplative) and Shabine the dramatic character (smuggler and brawler), 'The Schooner *Flight*' remains a major poem, containing virtually all the main themes of literature: imagination, history, exile, love and death. Below the engaging narrative it is philosophically profound – consider, for example, that unforgettable couplet: 'I try to forget what happiness was/and when that don't work, I study the stars.'

In it Walcott forges, from the diverse strands of his region's history – from the rhythms, intonations and syntax of West Indian dialect and the vocabulary and syntactical possibilities of Standard English – a poetic language that is musical, compressed and subtle.